UCD WOMEN'S CENTER

D0219220

I ANSWER WITH MY LIFE

Critical Social Thought

UCD WOMEN'S CENTER

Series editor: Michael W. Apple
Professor of Curriculum and Instruction and Educational Policy
  Studies, University of Wisconsin-Madison

Already Published

UCD WOMEN'S CENTER

I Answer With My Life
Life Histories of Women Teachers Working for Social Change

Kathleen Casey

ROUTLEDGE
New York • London

UCD WOMEN'S CENTER

Published in 1993 by

Routledge
29 West 35 Street
New York, NY 10001

Published in Great Britain by

Routledge
11 New Fetter Lane
London EC4P 4EE

Copyright © 1993 by Routledge, Inc.

An earlier version of Chapter 3 was published as "Teachers and Values: The Progressive Use of Religion in Education" in *Journal of Curriculum Theorizing*, Vol. 9, No. 1 (Spring, 1989), 23–69.

Printed in the United States of America on acid free paper.

All rights reserved. No part of this book may be reprinted or reproduced or utilized in any form or by any electronic, mechanical or other means, now known or hereafter invented, including photocopying and recording, or in any information storage or retrieval system, without permission in writing from the publishers.

Library of Congress Cataloging-in-Publication Data

Casey, Kathleen, 1944–
    I answer with my life : life histories of women teachers working
for social change / Kathleen Casey.
        p.   cm. — (Critical social thought)
    Includes bibliographical references (p.) and index.
    ISBN 0-415-90402-1 — ISBN 0-415-90403-X (pbk.)
    1. Women teachers—United States—History. 2. Catholic teachers—
United States—History. 3. Jewish Teachers—United States—History.
4. Afro-American teachers—History. 5. Oral history. 6. Critical
pedagogy—United States. 7. Feminist theory. 8. Education—Social
aspects—United States. I. Title. II. Series.
LB2837.C37   1993
371.1'0042—dc20   92-27507
                                                     CIP

British Library Cataloguing-in-Publication Data also available.

UCD WOMEN'S CENTER

To Makeba

We are together, my child and I. Mother and child, yes, but sisters really, against whatever denies us all that we are.

Alice Walker

UCD WOMEN'S CENTER

UCD WOMEN'S CENTER

Contents

UCD WOMEN'S CENTER

Acknowledgments

The teachers whose words appear in this work are, in a very special way, its primary authors. If they had not trusted me with their life stories, this book simply would not exist. To all these women, I give enormous thanks.

My daughter Makeba has shared the trials and tribulations of graduate school and of book-writing. In this sense, she is also one of the co-authors of this volume. So are the other members of my family who have contributed all kinds of assistance throughout the long and difficult process. I am grateful to them all.

Michael Apple has been, and will continue to be, family, friend, mentor, and colleague. Without his intellectual questioning, political understanding, and affectionate caring, this project could not have developed in the way it did. He gave it ground to stand on, and its success is a tribute to him.

Teachers and students, colleagues and friends have helped bring this book into being. Particular thanks go to Ron Aminzade, Karen Anijar, Rima Apple, Nicholas Appleton, Janet Barr, Iva Boslough, Michael Burawoy, Jim Carmichael, Ann Devaney, Maureen Dolan, Carole Edelsky, Guillermina Ellissondo, Elizabeth Ellsworth, Roger Hazoumé, Hannah Hill, Karen Holden, Jan Jipson, Sue Jungck, Margot Kennard, Mike King, Herbert Kliebard, Nancy Knupfer, Bea Kovacs, Susan Laird, Delores Liston, Lynda Moss, Irene Serna and Bruce Tomlinson,

I Answer With My Life

Joyce Shanks, Dorothee Soelle, Judy Stewart, Cate and Bob Weinberg, Bernard and Debby Young, and Ken Zeichner.

My colleagues in Curriculum and Educational Foundations, UNCG, Svi Shapiro, David Purpel, Fritz Mengert, and Chiranji Sharma, need to be remembered, as does Jeannette Dean, departmental secretary and much more. For helping me to understand what it is I am trying to say, I thank all my students at the University of North Carolina at Greensboro.

I am grateful to the Graduate School at the University of Wisconsin for a research travel grant which allowed me to collect teachers' narratives in three cities in the northeastern United States.

Finally, I thank Jayne Fargnoli at Routledge for reminding me to maintain my own voice. It made all the difference.

Series Editor's Introduction

We have entered a period of reaction in education. Our educational institutions are seen as failures. High drop-out rates, a decline in "functional literacy" (Kaestle, *et al.*, 1991), a loss of standards and discipline, the failure to teach "real knowledge," and more—all of these are charges levelled at schools and their teachers. And all of these, we are told, have led to declining economic productivity, a loss of international competitiveness, unemployment, poverty, and so on. Return to a romanticized "common culture" (Apple and Christian-Smith, 1991; Apple, 1990), make schools more efficient, more competitive, more open to private initiative; this will solve our problems.

As I have claimed elsewhere, such assertions place the blame on schools for conditions over which they have little control. This enables dominant groups to deflect a crisis often created by their own decisions onto schools and teachers. Equally as important is the fact that behind this is also an attack on egalitarian norms and values. Though hidden in the rhetorical flourishes of the critics, in essence "too much democracy"—culturally and politically—is seen as one of the major causes of "our" declining economy and culture (Apple, 1985; Apple, 1993). The threat to egalitarian ideals and to our very sense of social justice that this presents is never made explicit since it is always couched in the discourse of improving standards and quality in our educational system.

The Right wishes to bring us a new educational "market" guided by "freedom" and "choice." Yet these are really code words for a situation in which we can realistically expect that freedom and choice will be for those who can afford them and diversity in schools will be a polite way of describing educational apartheid (Green, 1991, p. 30).

This is not the first time our educational system has faced withering attacks from the Right. Nor is it the first time that teachers, for example, have been attacked ideologically or educationally. Many policies and practices in schools in fact do need serious questioning, but largely *because* of their basically rightist and a critical character. However, the concerted nature of these attacks and the power of the right-wing coalition that stands behind them makes this a particularly dangerous time, especially for those teachers at all levels who care deeply about creating more democratic policies and practices inside schools, between schools and their communities, and in society as a whole.

Even though many of the recent spate of national reports on education in the United States had a few teacher representatives involved, by and large the voices of teachers have been largely silenced. Even more difficult to hear have been the voices of politically active teachers.

Rest assured that there were and are many such teachers, teachers who in their daily lives constantly act against the racism and the patriarchal and class relations that tend to dominate all too many of our institutions. This very fact makes *I Answer With My Life* such a significant book. It enables us to listen to, and learn from, the lives of a number of teachers who constantly provide reminders of the very possibility of difference.

We want to begin by situating the "stories" that Kathleen Casey tells into the politics of the conservative restoration. Thus, the context is set by the ideological conditions in the larger society. Like her, we could ask, in a time of conservative triumphalism how can we conceive of social change? One of the answers she finds is in listening to the teachers who have not only asked this question, but—through their concrete actions—have answered it over the course of their entire lifetimes.

These are *women* teachers. And this is crucial to our understanding of how they interpret and act on the world. Nearly 67 percent of teachers overall and 87 percent of elementary school teachers are women. A sense of history would be useful here. Teaching has always played a major role in the lives of formally educated women. For example, as late as 1970 in the United States, 53 percent of women college graduates who were in the paid labor market taught at one time or other at the elementary or secondary level (Carter, 1989, p. 57).

Going back even further historically, by the end of the nineteenth century, a considerable number of educational and community leaders had become convinced that teaching was "women's true profession." It was an extension of and preparation for their role as wife and mother. While women had to struggle to open up teaching and continued to fight to gain recognition of their skills and power, teaching was very often seen by educational authorities as a way station for many women before they took up their "real" domestic vocation (Fraser, 1989, pp. 131–132). This, of course, was used to justify incredibly low pay, exploitative working and living conditions, a lack of autonomy and respect, and so on. Yet it also established a terrain of further conflict that continues to this day, for many women teachers had to engage in constant action—both overtly politicized and on an informally day-to-day level—to contest the content they were asked to teach and the goals they were asked to reach but had little say in formulating. It meant that there would be similar actions on how one should be with children, on the ethics of teaching and evaluation, and on the very control of one's daily life in and out of schools (Apple, 1988).

Thus, for women teachers, the personal has always been the political, in part because of the history of the ways teachers have been regulated in both their public and private lives.

Some of these beliefs about the "suitability" of women as teachers were contradicted by other patriarchal assumptions. Thus, in 1915 one male educator joined a chorus of other conservative commentators by warning that "The farmer that uses his land for golf-links and deer preserves instead of for crops has but one agricultural fate; the civilization that uses its women for stenographers, clerks and school-teachers instead of mothers has but one racial fate" (Clifford, 1989, p. 305). Resting his arguments on his own eugenic position, Edward Thorndike wrote, at approximately the same time, that hiring women teachers would result in "the prevention of gifted and devoted women from having and rearing children of their own flesh and blood" (Clifford, 1989, p. 305). The "biological welfare of the white race" and of the social classes who were "appropriately" in advantaged positions was at stake here. As a magazine for school executives noted in its statement against hiring married women as teachers, "It leads almost necessarily to childless homes or to the restriction of children in homes that really should produce more children. Every time you elect a married teacher, you tacitly endorse and encourage such practices which are the most reprehensible sins of the upper and middle classes" (Clifford, 1989, p. 305).

Thus, it was a woman's duty—both biologically and ideologically—to protect her class and race. She could do this by having children or she could do this in classrooms by ensuring that her students learned what was "essential" to their "proper position" in a hierarchal society. Needless to say, while this was not accepted by all women or by all women teachers, it did make it difficult for those teachers who had more democratic and critical sentiments. The conflict continued.

If the public and private lives of many white women teachers have involved a history of contesting such assumptions, this is true tenfold for African-American women teachers. We are just beginning to get a fuller picture of their lives, their often unbelievable working conditions, their own sacrifices and struggles in the face of conditions that seemed to be organized to prevent their success (Perkins, 1989). One of Kathleen Casey's accomplishments is to make the more recent daily struggles of African-American women teachers visible.

All of this is crucial, in part because it helps break down a common stereotype surrounding teachers. Women teachers have rarely been the one-dimensional and uniformly apolitical creatures portrayed by many of the male researchers who have studied their lives. Only by a more thorough understanding of their material conditions inside *and* outside of schools and only by seeing the gender, race, class, and religious dynamics that position them in such complex ways can this be made more clear (Casey and Apple, 1989; Apple, 1988; Apple, 1993).

As Casey puts it, "Women teachers' own understanding and interpretation of their experiences have been, until very recently, not only unrecorded, but actually silenced." In opposition to this, Casey enables us to see women teachers as authors of their own life history narratives, as "authors of their own lives," and, just as importantly, as authors of social change.

It is the group biography that takes center stage here. Behind it is the recognition that "no utterance in general can be attributed to the speaker exclusively; it is the product of the interactions of the interlocution, and broadly speaking, the product of the whole complex social situation in which it occurred."

Three groups of teachers speak in these pages. Some are white, some are African-American. Some are deeply religious, some are just as deeply secular. Yet each is committed to social justice and to the creation of the conditions both in education and in the larger society that would enable a less exploitative and more democratic and caring set of social arrangements to be built.

Casey's method is deceptively simple, though grounded theoretically in quite a sophisticated way. A simple request is given: "Tell me the story of your life." In her compelling narratives, this becomes something of more social significance. For the women teachers transform it into a response to the question "What is the meaning of your life?"

xiv

Life history is important here, since in many ways its task is to give history back to people in their own words. In the process, by giving the past back, it helps us in making our own futures. Of course, oral history and life history, by enabling people to tell their own lives with all of the selectivities and silences this entails, does not necessarily guarantee that people will "make their own futures" in transformative ways. Nor does it guarantee that relations of power will not be reconstituted in the ways "researchers" and "tellers" interact. Thus, the politics of life history is complicated. Casey provides a model for democratically working with teachers so that they are not silenced, and in the process helps us see new ways in which nonexploitative research can be carried on.

Drawing on Bakhtin's theories of language, Casey provides us with a picture of women teachers who are not only creations of discourse but *makers* of discourse. "Unlike the alienated personas of post-modern discourse, this self is not a jumble of fragments; she can articulate her own coherence. Acting within the limitations constructed by the other, she nevertheless has some choice, and she has some power." Casey's own words describe this. Placed side by side, the narratives of these groups of progressive teachers "create a kind of Bakhtinian dialogue on the possibilities of alternative discourse; together they stand in opposition to dominant interpretations of the meaning of education."

As she goes on to say, "Authored in the obscurity of nameless educational institutions, the life histories of these . . . women remind us of the extraordinary theoretical and practical powers of *ordinary* teachers and their students." What makes this book such an important one is clear in Casey's own reflections on the meanings of these women's lives. "All educators working for social change have a great deal to learn from the care these women give to their students; the outrage they feel towards injustice, and the way they dare to use the limited powers that they have."

After reading the moving personal narratives that provide the core of *I Answer With My Life,* I am certain that you will agree. And, perhaps, together with these teachers we can continue to answer with *our* own lives and act against those for whom greed and profit are the organizing principles of a society seemingly bent on ignoring the realities and futures of so many of its children.

Michael W. Apple
The University of Wisconsin, Madison

References

Apple, M. W. 1985. *Education and Power*. New York: Routledge.

Apple, M. W. 1988. *Teachers and Texts*. New York: Routledge.

Apple, M. W. 1990. *Ideology and Curriculum*. (2nd ed.) New York: Routledge.

Apple, M. W. 1993. *The Politics of Official Knowledge*. New York: Routledge.

Apple, M. W. & Christian-Smith, L. (eds.) 1991. *The Politics of the Textbook*. New York: Routledge.

Carter, S. B. 1989. "Incentives and Rewards to Teaching," in D. Warren (ed.), *American Teachers*. New York: Macmillan, pp. 49–62.

Casey, K. & Apple, M. W. 1989. "Gender and the Conditions of Teachers' Work," in S. Acker (ed.), *Teachers, Gender and Careers*. Philadelphia: Falmer Press, pp. 171–186.

Clifford, C. J. 1989. "Man/Woman/Teacher," in D. Warren (ed.), *American Teachers,* pp. 293–343.

Fraser, J. 1989. "Agents of Democracy," in D. Warren (ed.), *American Teachers,* pp. 118–156.

Green, A. 1991. "The peculiarities of English Education," in Education Group II (eds.), *Education Limited*. London: Unwin Hyman, pp. 6–30.

Kaestle, C., *et al.* 1991. *Literacy in the United States*. New Haven: Yale University Press.

Perkins, L. M. 1989. "The History of Blacks in Teaching," in D. Warren (ed.), *American Teachers,* pp. 344–369.

What is it that guarantees the internal connection between the elements of personality? Only the unity of responsibility. For what I have experienced and understood, . . . I answer with my life.

Mikhail Bakhtin

1

Introduction

Imagine that, through some sophisticated communication system, you could hear every word spoken on the subject of American education over the last several years. Millions of utterances would simultaneously enter your ears, creating an unbelievable babble.

But, suppose that some remarkable unscrambling device allowed you to begin to sort out these voices. Then you would certainly hear echoes of a particular set of sentences—being outlined by Glenn Seaborg, a Nobel laureate in chemistry; being drafted by Gerald Holton, Harvard physicist; being debated by members of a national commission on Excellence in Education; and being "printed millions of times and in a host of languages" (Olson, 1988: 1)—the opening lines of *A Nation at Risk:*

> If an unfriendly foreign power had attempted to impose on America the mediocre educational performance that exists today, we might well have viewed it as an act of war. As it stands, we have allowed this to happen to ourselves. . . . We have, in effect, been committing an act of unthinking, unilateral educational disarmament. (National Commission on Excellence in Education, 1983: 1)

You would also probably pick up the sound of the Secretary of Education, William Bennett, proposing solutions to this crisis: "Hire principals who are tough. Get serious about the use of class time. Nobody's for mindless school work in elementary classes. We have to find out who is in charge of the schools" (Bennett in Posner, 1986: 14).

If your auditory system allowed you to listen more carefully, however, you would begin to realize that these were the loudest, but not the only, voices. In the background, for example, you might be able to hear a faint chorus of children, singing in playgrounds, "Watch the schoolhouse burn to ashes. . . ."[1]

If you had access to different, less powerful, wavelengths, you would be able to catch the voices of anonymous women teachers. You could hear them discussing the schools in which they work.[2]

> And the reason I left was that I didn't agree with a lot of the philosophy in the school. I really believe that a school is a place where people come together, and form some kind of community, and it's *not* a prison, and if it's likened to anything, it's likened to a family rather than a prison. And my experience in that school was that it was *much* closer to a prison.

You could tune in on them talking about the students they teach.

> There were times when I said, "if you skip my class, I'm coming down to the mall to get you." So sometimes, I would go down to the mall, and it would be a big scene because the class would be waiting there, anticipating my coming back with these six-feet, you know, men. And I would get down to the mall, and I would say, "Hi, John!" "Uh, *Hi!*" You know. They were always really surprised. I said, "Well, we come to get you." And they looked, "We?"

And, you could listen to their political ideas.

> There isn't a good term for those of us who sort of. . . . You know . . . are still motivated by the civil rights agenda! You know, the unfinished agenda of those years. And that's how I identify myself. As one of the people who's still motivated by that unfinished agenda.

There are indeed millions of words on the subject of education in the air these days. But the flurry of discussion is not as chaotic as it might seem. The style of particular speakers is not merely idiosyncratic, and the attention paid to specific proposals is neither unpredictable nor arbitrary. The ongoing educational debate, as I show in this book, is a struggle over meaning, one in which, based on their own experiences, particular social groups formulate their own understandings and interpretations of education, and try to put their own values into practice.

This is, therefore, a work about language, politics and education in contemporary America. It is based on the premise that language and politics are inextricably intertwined. Language is here simply defined as the way in which human beings make meaning, as well as the worldviews which have been socially constructed in that process, while politics are understood as relationships between groups with different worldviews, and the processes by which they contest each others' perspectives. And these contestations are not limited to the verbal level; my definitions assume that words and deeds, policy and practice, are also inseparably linked.

As we know, some of the most intense, even violent, social battles in American history have been fought over schools; within living memory, we have not only seen national guard troops standing at the schoolhouse door in Arkansas, we have watched soldiers shoot students on American college campuses. The Civil Rights Movement and the Vietnam War appear in this work; so does Vatican II, and the launching of Sputnik, all in connection with educational issues. But each of these events has a different degree and kind of importance in the discourses of the particular social groups who talk about them. In the conventionally political sphere, as well as in the politics of knowledge, different social groups in this country speak distinctive languages for valuing education.

In a deliberate reversal, I move the most prominent speakers in the contemporary struggle over education to the edges of my analysis.[3] This marginalization is meant not to underestimate, but rather to undermine the overpowering influence of dominant conservative discourse. At the center of my study are ordinary, anonymous authors whose ideas have, until now, only been known in their immediate social circles. The purpose of this book is to celebrate their alternative progressive versions of education, and in doing so, to recreate the possibility of public debate which has actually been suppressed by the national reports.

Of course, we cannot expect to see progressive perspectives on education praised by their adversaries. But it almost seems at times as if they did not actually exist. Although it has regularly been described as a national debate on education, the ideological initiative started by *A Nation at Risk,* and sustained by subsequent national reports, has never taken the form of a dialogue. Indeed, even the various voices which were solicited at scheduled public hearings have been silenced by the self-described "strident" (Seaborg in Olson, 1988: 22) assertions of the written reports.

One of the teachers who will speak in a later chapter told me she appeared before one of these panels; another prepared a document for a child advocacy group to present as testimony. Yet I cannot hear these women's descriptions of children living in poverty in any of these reports. The voices of teachers have been systematically edited out; a handful of token representatives have been unable to prevent the development of a regulatory and punative posture, as each successive report seems more concerned with evaluation and enforcement.

Women teachers' own understandings and interpretations of their experiences have been, until very recently, "not only unrecorded, but actually silenced" (Popular Memory Group, 1982: 210), in educational literature, as well as in the larger public domain.[4] This book represents one attempt to remedy that situation. In Chapters Three, Four and Five, women teachers are presented as authors—of their own life history narratives, of their own lives, and, of social change.

Chapter Two sets the scene for the presentation of my original research and analysis in subsequent chapters by situating that work within a theoretical, methodological and political context. I show how the ideas of the Popular Memory Group have influenced my collection of the oral history narratives of women teachers, and how Bakhtin's theories are important for my analysis of these texts. I discuss the actual procedures employed in planning and implementing this project, and I consider the social relations of research. This chapter also outlines an overarching model for understanding the multiplicity and diversity of various discourses on education in both contemporary and historical contexts.

In-depth analyses of three groups of teacher-generated texts are presented. In Chapter Three, the narratives of Catholic women religious, nuns, are introduced; these women have taught in parochial schools, and have been politically involved in "social justice ministry." Chapter Four concentrates on the life histories of secular Jewish women, who have taught in inner-city schools, and whose political projects are connected with the "Old" and "New" Left. In Chapter Five, the stories of black women teachers are presented; their personal, professional, and political lives are committed to "the uplift of the race."

In each of these chapters, individual teachers' narratives have been examined for constructions common to the group, and these patterns have been assembled in the form of a discourse, a consistent system of

4

controlling metaphors, notions, categories, and norms which develop and delimit its speakers' conceptions. Teachers' self-identities are considered, as are their assessments of the institutions within which they have worked, and their relationships with the children they have taught.

In the concluding chapter, I situate these speakers' narratives within the progressive traditions to which they refer, and I discuss the theoretical significance and the practical importance of these women's life histories in a time of conservative triumphalism. Hopefully, by the time readers have finished this work, they will have a clearer understanding of the ways in which various social groups in this country talk about education; they will be able to place the several quotations which begin this introduction into their ideological contexts; and they will be able to situate *themselves* relative to the political perspectives which have been discussed.

2

Theory, Methodology, and Politics in Discourse Collection and Analysis

In the metaphor which introduces this study, I imagine the reader of this book as part of an audience tuned in on recent pronouncements on American education. But listening or reading, are not passive, neutral activities. We engage in a dialogue, whether we are in an actual conversation with another person, or watching the television, or reading a newspaper. While we read or listen, we continually make judgments on what we see or hear; we make sense through a process of selection and rejection. And what we select and reject very much depends on who we are, who is speaking to us, what they say, how they say it, where and when we are listening.

In this chapter I identify myself as a researcher and I locate my research project in a specific social context at a particular moment in time. I briefly discuss the ways in which my own personal, professional and political experiences have shaped, and have subsequently been shaped by, this book. I situate myself theoretically, acknowledging my intellectual debts to the Popular Memory Group and Mikhail Bakhtin; and I describe the actual procedures I have used in the collection and analysis of the narratives in this book. I also comment upon the ways in which participants actively influenced both my procedures and my final conclusions.

My Own Identity As a Woman Teacher Working for Social Change

Let me introduce my discussion of the theory, methodology and politics of this research project with a brief life story, one which focuses on the ways in which my own modes of interpretation have been influenced by my personal relationships and lived experiences. I should begin by saying that I come from a family of teachers, seven at the last count, including myself. I tell my students I was genetically determined to be a teacher!

My father was teacher-as-worker.[5] He taught in an all-boys' vocational high school, and was employed as a skilled draftsman and sheet-metalworker in school vacations. I remember my father boasting that he could make "square into round" ducts, complaining about the Board of Education ("One Ten Livingston Street"), and bringing home stickers which said: "I am an underpaid New York City schoolteacher." Because my childhood coincided with a particularly intense period of labor history, I recall the angry suspense of teachers' and sheet-metalworkers' strikes, my father at home, hammering plasterboard, or mixing cement, arguing with the news on the radio.

Yet this is not an uncontradictory set of memories: my father building the United Nations one summer; teenage boys breaking their teachers' windshields with baseball bats; my father's endless evening classes at City College, because he did not have a college degree; union medical benefits paying for my open-heart surgery; sheet-metalworkers' union scholarships contributing to my siblings' college tuition; and that same union being forced by the Supreme Court to admit black apprentices.

My mother engaged in "labors of love": creating family; being pregnant; mothering six children, which included keeping the sickly one (me) alive; making children's and dolls' clothes (which I can still describe in minute detail); really cooking; always cleaning; washing and hanging out clothes to dry. When I was in second grade, hearing the squeak of clothesline pulleys outside the classroom window made me homesick.

My mother always worked; she always taught; but, before she was married, and after my youngest sister went to school, she was paid wages to teach other people's children. My mother worked in the school with the lowest reading scores in New York City. Sometimes children were only enrolled for one month, until the rent came due. Her students came to school in December without jackets. Families were constantly getting burned out of their apartments. The administrative solution was prepackaged curriculum; "dis star, dat star," I mocked it.

These were my mother's other children. At home she told us stories about their lives. One year she had a girl she called "my black Kathleen." As long as I can remember, my mother cared about poor children. I cannot recall exactly what my mother said as we rode on the elevated train, looking through cracked windows into apartments of black and Puerto Rican families. Was it then that we talked about migrant farm workers' children, and Janey Larkin's blue willow plate (Gates, 1940)?

When I worked in the Headstart Program in Bedford Stuyvesant, I came home with stories too. I found out about Ebony magazine when the black teacher with whom I worked showed it to her class. There was a silent, watchful little girl; one day she surprised every one by talking into a toy telephone. There was a little boy who did not know what crayons were for. I can still remember Sandra, the two Deborahs and Enrique after twenty-five years; when my (black) daughter visits the high school where my brother works, and meets the young black women he teaches, I wonder what those young people are doing now.

At the same time that I was learning about the lives of Jewish and black school teachers, black and Puerto Rican students in the New York City public schools, I was being taught how to be Catholic during my sixteen years of parochial education. A curious mixture of memories here: fifty children in a class, some of them "displaced persons" from Germany; my sister joining the convent; studying Latin, Greek and the history of Western Civilization; wanting to be a Maryknoll missionary; Cardinal Spellman's real estate; Jack Kennedy, one of our boys, elected, and assassinated; drinking sassafras tea at the Catholic Worker; my brother working with the Berrigans against the war in Vietnam, and with Cesar Chavez for the farm workers' strike. Sister Francis Paula used to say you could never stop being Catholic; when I heard Philip Berrigan speak during the war against Iraq, I was Catholic again.

After many years living overseas and in other areas of this country, it has been interesting to rediscover the roots of these practically primordial passions. Indeed, my own experiences may have provided impetus for this project, but, in a more than reciprocal return, my study of the life histories of other teachers has given me an opportunity to reflect upon my own teaching, and to explore the social grounding of my own ideas.

Planning the Project

Always much more than a doctoral dissertation, the actual formulation of this research project nevertheless began when I was in graduate school. As I proceeded with my studies, a number of interesting questions about teachers began to emerge: Why are teachers regularly maligned in public discourse? Why does so much of academic literature "blame the teacher?" How do teachers differ from each other? How are teachers influenced by the students they teach? What is the relationship between teaching and the social environment of the teacher? What is the relationship between teaching and the rest of a teacher's life? What is the relationship between teaching and a teacher's political values? and so forth. It seemed to me from the beginning that the most pressing of these issues, and the one which was perhaps held the key to all the others, was the relationship between teaching and political action in the lives of ordinary teachers.

Several sets of readings[6] in various graduate courses proved to be particularly influential in the final conceptualization of my research. "Classical" sociological studies of teachers were a negative impetus. Although they had been written only a short time before, by the early eighties when I was reading them, Dreeben (1970) and Lortie (1975) appeared conspicuously masculinist in their analyses of women's work. They were also clearly anti-union. *Pace* Lortie, I was not conservative, and I did not want to be relegated to an endnote. From the other side of the political spectrum, my readings of such writers as Willis (1977), with their "not yet fully conscious" assessment of their subjects, and corresponding grim evaluation of the political "potential" of the Left, also made me want to focus on progressive *activism*.

At the same time, a class assignment alerted me to the possibilities of in-depth interviews with teachers. In another course, I was introduced to the oral history debates, and became convinced that this was the methodology I had been looking for. This conclusion was confirmed in yet another class, where actual quotations from women teachers, discovered in a preliminary report on life history interviews by Dee Ann Spencer (later published as a book in 1986) proved to be the most exciting words I had ever read on the subject of teachers.

Throughout the eighties, a different kind of academic research was gaining momentum, one which invited the interpretations of groups largely ignored by traditional historians. My own initial attraction to oral history was fueled by those versions connected with socialist, feminist and civil rights projects. From its inception, then, this book has been based on a particular understanding of research, one in which theory, methodology, and politics are interrelated, and oriented towards progressive ends. History itself is "a ground of political struggle," the Popular Memory Group (1982: 214) insist, and putting the working class, including people of color and women, on its agenda has the potential to change the very terms of their struggle. In Thompson's (1978: 226) words: "Oral history gives history back to the people in their own words. And in giving a past, it also helps them towards a future of their own making."

Working-class subjects, however, do not inevitably guarantee a radical history (White, 1981; Popular Memory Group, 1982). In the field of education, the use of life story and biography as methods for studying teachers' lives has continued to grow. Yet it has also become increasingly clear that "some leftist scholars have employed this methodology but so too have a large body of less overtly political scholars besides some of a conservative orientation" (Goodson, 1992: 9). Given the political consequences of current research, which seems to solicit teachers' understandings only to sit in judgment upon them, it is imperative to explain the ways in which my own project deals with the problems posed by the practice of oral history.

The Popular Memory Group

Oral history in all its various manifestations (for instance, popular memory, life history, personal narrative) is deeply entangled in current conflicts over theory, methodology and politics in academic research. Some proponents have spent considerable energy attempting to legitimate a "soft" method within a context of the "rigorous" standards of traditional historical research.[7] As practiced by some researchers, oral history does seem to be a simple methodology which accentuates "subjectivity"; but an appeal to "objectivity" is not the only solution to the problems this approach creates. At its most sophisticated level, oral history research can present a complex effort to reintegrate and realign ideas from historically prior frameworks.

In a chapter entitled "Popular memory: Theory, politics, and method," the Popular Memory Group (1982) presents what remains, in my own judgment, the single most important discussion of oral history research. Certainly the group's analysis has proven to be the most important influence on my own research, from the planning stage until the present day.

While acknowledging the dilemmas inherent in the present practice

11

of oral history, the Popular Memory Group argues that a positivist approach is wholly mistaken. To choose professional procedures and the canons of objectivity is to "limit the radical potential of oral history practice" (p. 221). The costs of the positivist solution are high (pp. 224–225). The historian-researcher is systematically privileged as a bearer of the scientific canon, and cultural determinations and effects are rendered quite marginal. The culture of the historian is made invisible; the relations of power in the social relations of research are neglected.

The culturally constructed character of the sources themselves are also disguised (p. 225). They are seen only as bearers of fact, and little concern is given to their cultural frameworks of meaning. At its worst, this results in an obsession with problems of bias, distortion and the "trustworthiness" of sources. This is unfortunate because of the strong tendency for "the practice of research (to) conform to (and deepen) social divisions which are also relations of power and inequality" (pp. 219). Class relations between working-class people and sections of the professional middle class ought to be based on a more equal alliance; such alliances have been crucial in the history of left-wing politics (p. 220).

Relational Analysis in Oral History

Relational analysis is the key notion in the Popular Memory Group's own approach to oral history (p. 211). What is most important is neither the "objective" (structure) nor the "subjective" (culture), but the relationship between them; neither past nor present, but the relationship between them; neither dominant memory nor commonplace understandings, but the relationship between them; neither the personal/individual nor large-scale changes, but the relationship between them.

The relationship between the structural and the cultural readings of oral history can turn out to be one of congruence or confirmation or surprises or modifications or extensions, or it can be one of slippage. "Factual disparities" or discontinuities between structural and cultural readings become, in the Popular Memory Group's alternative epistemology, sources of valuable insight, not problems of distortion (pp. 229–230).

Luisa Passerini, cited by the Popular Memory Group (pp. 229–230), provides a dramatic example of slippage: members of the Italian working class, when asked "What do you remember of the period before the last war?" gave irrelevant and inconsistent answers. They told jokes, recited whole life stories without any reference to fascism, and left chronological gaps of twenty years in their lives. The "bare facts" of Italian history could not begin to give us an understanding of fascism in the way their combination with these oral histories offers to do. "This self-censorship is evidence of a scar, a violent annihilation of many years in human life, a profound wound in daily experience" (Passerini in Popular Memory Group, p. 230).

The principal value of oral history is that its information comes complete with evaluations, explanations and theories, with selectivities and silences, which are intrinsic to its representation of reality (Popular Memory Group, p. 228). Oral history, read in all its rich wholeness, will illuminate conscious human activity in a way positivism never can.

So it was that I began my research alerted to the importance of teachers' own understandings of their experiences (even though all the implications of this proposition were not completely clear at first). That these narratives were not elicited simply for the "information" which could be extracted must be credited to the Popular Memory Group; that teachers' "interpretations" were considered to be equally, and possibly more, valuable components, can be attributed to my acquaintance with their work. With the same attention to cultural frameworks of meaning, I have included my own autobiographical statements throughout this book.

Assembling the Subjects

The alternative content of oral history does not guarantee transformative practice; the relations of power between researcher and resource persons are even more important (Popular Memory Group, p. 223; Lather, 1991). A fundamental example of the researcher's power is, of course, the establishment of criteria for inclusion and exclusion of subjects. This process becomes particularly delicate when political "qualifications" are involved. In my own case, the identification of both "progressive" and "activist" teachers proved problematical, even from the planning stage.

In my original proposal, I wrote that these women "will be identified as "progressive" "because they advocate social change which will benefit deprived constituencies, and they recognize conflicts, contradictions and inequalities in society." I also wrote that, in a second stage

13

of interviewing (the first stage was to be open-ended), they would answer questions on their political activities, "including their membership in organizations, their self-identification, their curriculum work, and their life-styles." In fact, I never did make a list of actual organizations. My minimalist formula was a compromise between an intuitive resistance to exclusionary strictures, and the pressure I felt to provide some sort of "proof" which distinguished these teachers from conservative ones.

My initial caution was reinforced by expediency. Even if I had wanted to do so, "leaving out 'liberal' women" (as some of my peers suggested) did not seem feasible when I could not find any women who would call themselves "radical" or "communist." For that matter, most of the women I interviewed didn't call themselves "liberal" either. Some women even refused the "political" label, although they had been enthusiastically identified as "activists" by others. The more interviewing that went on, the more ambiguous the issue of political naming became.

I have explained, with more specificity, in the introductions to Chapters Three, Four and Five, some of the ways in which this problem was partially solved. In a general sense, it is clear that the problems I encountered in assembling and analyzing these life histories have eroded any tendencies I ever had towards definitive definitions and orthodox tenets. The theoretical justifications of my present position are presented in this chapter; the consequences should be clear throughout the book. I am now convinced that (1) living persons do not conform to abstract definitions, that (2) the contemporary progressive political scene is diffuse and diverse, and that (3) I did find a good sampling of the progressive teachers who were "out there."

In order to find women teachers who were progressive political activists, I told everyone I knew, in those precise words, that I was looking for such persons. Almost every one I spoke to seemed to have a taken-for-granted understanding of what this meant, for they rarely asked questions, and usually immediately began to give me names and tell me stories. I asked my family and friends for referrals; I told everyone I knew in the school of education, teachers I met in the course of my work, people I met at political gatherings. I phoned two teachers I read about in the newspaper.

The Sample

My first set of interviews were conducted in one large and one smaller city in the midwestern United States. While they were still going on, I decided to extend my sampling geographically to see whether different social environments were characterized by distinctive kinds of educational and political activities. I then travelled to a large city with an already established, politically oriented teachers group, a large city with a majority "minority" school population, and another smaller city, all in the northeastern United States. The exact locations were determined by my limited money and time, as well as the number of contacts I could find. Although my travels were limited to these two areas, some of the women in the study had spent long periods of their lives in the southern and western United States. The alternative regional perspectives which can be glimpsed in their narratives only reinforces my ideas about the distinctive political configurations of contrasting social environments.

From the start I had chosen to interview only women, both because women constitute the majority of teachers, and because I was interested in the influence of feminism on contemporary women teachers' lives. And, from the beginning, I was determined to include black, as well as white, women teachers, since black teachers have been an almost totally neglected group, and one which I expected would include a number of activists. In the Northeast, I was able to contact Jewish women teachers for the first time; they, of course, became a crucial part of this study. As I have noted elsewhere, religion was the unexpected "variable" which appeared in the course of the interviews themselves.

By the time I finished, I had recorded the narratives of thirty-three women. This collection of life histories contained a sampling based on the qualities listed above. It also included examples of a very wide range of progressive political activities; when in doubt, I erred in the direction of inclusivity. And, as it turned out, twenty women had taught in elementary schools, and twenty in secondary; the overlap of levels included a number of women who had worked at the elementary, secondary, and college levels.

The Prospectus

While I preferred to invite women either in person or by telephone, I wrote to those at a long distance. The following excerpts from the letters I sent are indicative of the kind of information I provided to prospective sources.

—has given me your name as a person who would be very good to include in my research project on life histories of politically progressive women teachers, so I am writing to make a formal invitation, and to give you some of the details.

I have enclosed a brief description of my project; it will show that not all women teachers are conservative, as some research suggests, and will describe the reasons why, and the ways in which some of them get involved in working for social change.

My interview format consists of a one hour session, in which you tell the story of your life in your own words, and another one or two hours in which you answer questions about your teaching experience and your political work. All participants will be anonymous, and will have access to drafts of my written work.

. . . I hope that all of our combined efforts will produce an important document about teachers, about women, and about progressive politics. . . .

The "brief description," which was given to all participants, read as follows:

Teachers are regularly criticized in the American public forum, yet research rarely allows them to voice their own concerns. This thesis will address some of the silences in the literature on teachers: (1) the conditions under which contemporary teachers (the majority of whom are women) work and live; (2) teachers' own understandings of their work, their lives and their society; (3) the ways in which teachers act to improve their own and others' conditions. Ordinary women who have been or are elementary or secondary school teachers will be solicited through personal networks. (Here I use the definitions quoted above.) Eighteen women, who presently reside in ———, ——— , ———, and ———, will tell their life stories in their own words, and answer questions on their political activities; six of these same women will also answer in-depth questions on the economic and cultural areas of their lives, and those of their families and students. Using historical sociology, this thesis will expand the analysis of teachers horizontally, to their whole lives, and vertically, to changes over time. It will look at the gender, race and class relations of women engaged in teaching, and relate their lives to relevant moments of contemporary labor history, history of education and histories of political mobilizations and organizations in the U.S.A.

I quote this xeroxed sheet in its entirety in order to make clear the framing within which the women in this study constructed their own stories. I do not expect that many of them studied it at great length, yet, it was my "first word" of the dialogue in which we would engage.

To my regret, certain features were all too well remembered. When I made the differentiation between the original eighteen and the "in-depth" six, I was only thinking of how much material I could possibly deal with. In the eyes of those who were to be interviewed, however, this distinction became a judgment of worth. Several women nervously inquired as to whether they would be included in the second group. Appalled by my shortsightedness, I assured them they could, if they wanted to be.

Collecting the Narratives

In actual practice, the interviews (mercifully) never came even close to the analytical neatness of this proposal. There were several reasons why this happened. The major cause was the sentence with which I opened the interviews: "Tell me the story of your life," a challenge which I followed with silence. This was the most open-ended way I could invent to elicit the selectivities of the subjects themselves, a goal I had set after reading the work of the Popular Memory Group. And it was extraordinarily successful in achieving that end, to my distress when faced with the job of analyzing what were, as a result, very un-rule-ly manuscripts.

The invitation to create a life history narrative was an extraordinary event for these women. Only two had even been involved in such a project before; neither had been anonymous in the other interviews, and so were wary of getting a "political reputation." Yet they could not resist the opportunity to talk about things that were so important to them, and once again to tell their stories to a usually indifferent world. For ordinary women who had never expected to write an autobiography, the life history narrative became a task with enormous personal meaning. And I became the intermediary, who could carry their intimate meanings into the public sphere. For this reason, and because the political nature of the project further reinforced the need for trust (reprisals were a real possibility for some women), the relationship between the research and subject was never, and indeed could not be, a formal one.

We often arranged to meet in the woman's own home, where she would serve me lunch, tea, or a bowl of ice cream. In fact, while I ate, *she* would be interviewing *me,* deciding what we had in common, and establishing the nature of the dialogue which would take place. Some common ground needed to be established, then the face-to-face encounter could proceed. Only by being an "insider," someone who identified with and sympathized with the person speaking, could I become part of this conversation. It is not surprising, therefore, that understanding the intense nature of this activity, several women refused to participate in the project.

Although I had actively solicited these women's own interpretations, at the same time, the priorities of academic research on teachers still lingered in my head; so I was continually startled while listening to the narratives. I was amazed when one woman began her story twenty years after her birth. I was shocked when another ended hers with the death of her first husband, fifteen years previously; her two-year-old daughter from a second marriage played in the next room. As a rule, husbands were barely mentioned in these narratives, a phenomenon I do not know how to interpret. The deaths of husbands, parents, and a daughter were of central significance in the stories in which they appeared; and death proved to be a central theme for one group of women, as I have noted elsewhere. So, the emphasis on teaching and politics cannot fully explain silences on some aspects of personal family life.

These narratives were "highly constructed texts" (Popular Memory Group, p. 228). The intensity with which these women told their stories and the coherence which developed as they spoke meant that they often ended with a strong sense of closure, one which I felt I could not violate by asking further questions. Yet I would feel frustrated because some of my questions were left unanswered; I particularly remember wondering about one woman's father's occupation after we had finished a particularly long series of conversations. It took some time for me to realize that I could not have it "both ways," to really understand the consequences of my chosen methodology.

There was one question, however, with which I almost always persisted because it was so surprising to the speaker and therefore so revealing of her political assumptions. "What," I would ask, "is the most radical thing you have ever done?" Here women would pause and take time to define the meaning of "radical"; sometimes they would generate multiple meanings, "theirs" versus "mine," or "adventuristic" versus "effective." The examples were remarkable, including taking part in physically dangerous demonstrations, writing curriculum, and leaving dog excrement on a boss' desk.

This question seemed to amuse many women and became one of the opportunities which some of them took to participate in a carnival-like freedom of expression, to enter (in Bakhtinian terms) that arena where unrestrained "nonlegitimated voices can compete with the ideologies of the status quo" (Quantz & O'Connor, 1988: 100). Many women were quite openly antagonistic to school, church and governmental authorities in their narratives, and, since our relationship was based on some kind of broadly defined political agreement, they felt free to express their antipathy in an uninhibited vocabulary, for instance, "bastard," "fuck-up," "shit." I do not wish to place undue emphasis on these parts of the narratives, but simply to acknowledge that mockery and laughter can be an important part of political expression.

Analyzing the Narratives

Throughout this book I refer to the life history narratives as texts. Of course it took many hours of transcription for them to be changed from tape recordings into that physical written form. I am grateful to Judy Stewart for this work, without which my analysis would have been impossible.

As my thinking about analysis developed, I found myself finally putting aside the idea of interrogating the texts using concepts from academic sociology. Sometimes I could not find a complete set of answers to such questions, because some women did not find it important to address, for example, the influence of their parents' occupations, or their own voting records, or which magazines they read. Using such a grid, furthermore, put me in danger of losing the most remarkable parts of these narratives, the pattern of their own priorities. I eventually derived these patterns from the texts themselves, using a broad framework based on Bakhtin's theory of discourses, together with models for the analysis of metaphors (Kliebard, 1975) and languages (Huebner, 1975) of curriculum.

While the Popular Memory Group's work guided my collection of teachers' oral histories, it was the work of Mikhail Bakhtin which gave shape to my analysis of these narratives. It would be interesting to study the commonalities between the Popular Memory group and the Bakhtin Circle, separated as they are by many years and miles, and yet clearly sharing an overlapping set of assumptions. For the moment I will simply observe that the thoughts of an obscure Russian theorist would not have been rediscovered if they did not resonate with those of some contemporary scholars.

Bakhtin's Theory of Language

"Perhaps Bakhtin's most radical contribution," according to G. S. Morson (1986: xi), "lies in his rethinking of traditional oppositions: of the individual to society, of self to other, of the specific utterance to the totality of language, and of particular actions to the world of norms and conventions." From certain points of view, such a rethinking would almost certainly be judged radical, although it might not be considered a contribution. By dissolving these dichotomies, a "method that, he believed, provided the only meaningful escape from an endless oscillation between dead abstractions" (Morson, p. xi), Bakhtin undercuts the very premises not only of much academic research but also of paradigm creators who describe, and thus reinforce, such divisions.

What Bakhtin wishes to show is that "analytic categories have been mistaken for social facts and that, in fact, apparent opposites are made up of the same material" (Morson, p. xi). Quantz and O'Connor (1988) make much of this point in their article advocating the use of Bakhtin's theories for "writing critical ethnography" in educational research. The results of traditional ethnography, according to Quantz and O'Connor, are "the reduction of cultural life to a static system of categorical relationships which leave untouched many critical factors involved in the construction of cultural exchanges" (p. 95).

In his "extraordinary sensitivity to the immense plurality of experience" (Holquist, 1981: xx), and in his celebration of the world's unpredictability (Clark and Holquist, 1984: 347), Bakhtin sets himself a more difficult task than most theorists do, but he also achieves a more inclusive understanding. This is accomplished through an overarching theory of "translinguistics" or "intertextuality," and, on the level of specificity, with the concept of "utterance." Thus, "language" can be said to be Bakhtin's central concept and controlling metaphor. But this is not linguistics in any technical or professional sense.

The Multiplicity of Languages

For Bakhtin, "language" is not understood in a general, singular or unitary sense; it is always defined in terms of diversity and changeability: "languages," "multiple voices," "heteroglossia." "Language is never unity," says Bakhtin; "actual social life and historical becoming create a multitude of concrete worlds, a multitude of bounded verbal-ideological and social belief systems" (Bakhtin, 1981: 288).

The plurality of social situations creates a multiplicity of languages, according to Bakhtin, for, like society, "a language is stratified not only into dialects in the strict sense of the word," but also "into languages that are socio-ideological," such as languages belonging to professions or generations. "This stratification and diversity of speech will spread wider and penetrate to even deeper levels as long as a language is alive and still in the process of becoming" (Bakhtin in Holquist, p. xix). So, for example, in this book the language of the teaching profession is further stratified by gender dialects, by religious dialects, and so forth.

The Intersection of Languages

In Bakhtin's relational analysis, however, while various social discourses have areas of divergence, they "do not exclude," "but rather intersect with each other" (Bakhtin, p. 291), as they encounter each other in small and larger scale social interactions, and as they struggle over meaning.

This is not evident in "traditional cultural descriptions," according to Quantz and O'Connor (pp. 99–100), for they

> are constructed by theorists from collections of formal, systemic vocalizations within the community, usually products of the ideologically powerful. They subsequently depict social change according to shifts in the dominant ideology of the culture. Attention is thus placed on the struggle of well-formed, major paradigms. Since these struggles tend to be between legitimated elites and not between the elites and the disempowered, this focus is quite the reverse of what is needed.

It is extremely important for researchers to create a Bakhtinian sense of the spatial coexistence and temporal simultaneity of all social languages in order to portray and encourage social dialogue:

> When analysis and description of history are combined with the spatial juxtaposition, the utterances of the disempowered

21

can be situated with the greater dialogue of the day. Subcul-
tures thus are not isolated from the powerful, their culture is
set into relation to the dominant cultures surrounding them;
they are not portrayed as outside of time, but seen in relation
to historical forces (Quantz and O'Connor, p. 105).

In this book, progressive activist teachers enter the dialogue of the day
as equal speakers. And the juxtaposition of their narratives to various
versions of the dominant culture surrounding them is quite remarkable.

The philosophical traditions of these teachers, expressed in academic
terms, turn out to be the antiphilosophical, anticonventional theoriz-
ings of *existentialism, pragmatism* and *signifying*. A comparison of
these teachers' controlling metaphors to those of public policy reports
reveals certain continuities, such as the construction of teacher as
worker; it also highlights the nuances of teachers' specific innovations,
in the reconstituted "partisan artisan." Hearing the voices of progressive nuns, we notice, perhaps for the first time, the suppression of
existential concerns in the dominant discourse; listening to the words
of black women teachers, and their retired white women colleagues, we
discover the disappearance of the teacher-as-mother in other teachers'
narratives, as well as in public policy debates.

Ordinarily, of course, the dialogue of the day is an unequal struggle.
Because language is "overpopulated with the intentions of others,"
"expropriating it, forcing it to submit to one's own intentions and
accents is a difficult and complicated process" (Bakhtin, p. 294). This
is clearly dramatized in the teachers' narratives, in the struggle over
naming recounted by Catholic nuns, for example. And the lament of
one Left activist, "I really feel as though the right has successfully coopted so much of our language," echoes Bakhtin's explanation: "all
socially significant worldviews have the capacity to exploit the inten-
tional possibilities of language." They are "capable of stratifying language in proportion to their social significance"; they are "capable of
attracting words and forms into their own orbit," and "to a certain
extent," capable of "alienating them from others" (Bakhtin, p. 290.

For Bakhtin, the dialogic relationship between languages is further
complicated by the way in which it can be extended historically both
backwards and forwards in time. As Clark and Holquist have pointed
out, even in his last published words, Bakhtin would not permit closure:

There is neither a first word nor a last word. The contexts of dialogue are without limit. They extend into the deepest past and
the most distant future. Even meanings both in dialogues of the

remotest past will never be finally grasped once and for all, for they will always be renewed in later dialogue. At any present moment of the dialogue there are great masses of forgotten meanings, but these will be recalled once again at a given moment in the dialogue's later course when it will be given new life. For nothing is absolutely dead: every meaning will someday have its homecoming festival (Bakhtin in Clark and Holquist, pp. 348, 350).

This historical sense can be found in the continuous reconstruction of teacher-as-professional from meanings generated by a previous reform movement (Casey and Apple, 1989). It can be seen in the way that post-Sputnik (fifties) arguments still engage (sixties) equity claims in (eighties) educational debates. The reconstitution of Catholic, Marxist and African-American traditions in the life history narratives are also part of this renewal process. Intriguingly, this sense of historical dialogue explains how the metaphor of artisan can have a "homecoming festival" in postindustrial discourse of inner-city teachers.

The Self Encounters the Other

The dialogue between social languages is, written large, the same kind of process which takes place, on a smaller scale, in face-to-face encounters. Just as each discourse is elaborated in relationship to other discourses around it, so, according to Bakhtin, it is only in relationship to the other that the self can be defined.

This necessary interdependence is described in a set of conversational metaphors. Simply by being other, the "other" challenges the "self": who are you? Then, replying to the demands of the social world, the self can demonstrate her "response-ability"; answering the questions of the social world, she can establish her own "author-ity." In Clark and Holquist's (p. 68) rendering, "what the self is answerable to is the social environment; what the self is answerable for is the authorship of its responses."

Bakhtin's theory of the subject is not only social; it is also fundamentally moral and political. Unlike Althusser's (1972) interpellated subject, this self is more than a creation of discourse; she can also be one of its makers. Unlike the alienated persona of post-modern discourse, this self is not a jumble of fragments; she can articulate her own coherence. Acting within the limitations constructed by the other, she nevertheless has some choice, and she has some power.

Each of us is "without an alibi in existence," according to Bakhtin (in Clark and Holquist, p. 64), and the justification for one's being can only be made through social words and deeds. My asking the women in this study to "tell me the story of your life" becomes an interrogation for social significance: "what is the meaning of your life?" In the histories of their lives, where political *naming, doing* and *(re)interpreting* create personal identity, as well as in the political act of telling those stories, these women acquit themselves. "What is it that guarantees the internal connection among the elements of personality? Only the unity of responsibility. For what I have experienced and understood, I answer with my life (Bakhtin in Morson, 1986: x).

Having been told, such a set of life histories challenge those to whom they speak, (but especially the person who solicited them) not to put them in double jeopardy, not to sit in public judgment upon them. It is with such a sense of their integrity and mine, that I have tried to conduct my analysis of these texts. The positive responses of those participants who have read drafts in which their words appear are encouraging.

The practical, analytical consequences of such a position include not only learning the language of the speakers, but also to a large extent, adopting it. Politically, it means articulating points of intersection, and discovering common ground. Indeed, the analogue for this kind of analysis is the political coalition. In contrast, while my analysis of dominant discourse (Casey, 1988a) may seem technically similar to my analysis of teachers' narratives (in both cases, I examine notions, metaphors, and so forth), it is fundamentally adversarial from a political point of view.

Framing the Text

In "Life histories and social change," Thompson (1981) describes life history and oral history as the same method; the first name, he explains, is simply the label given by sociologists; the second by historians. From my perspective, life history narratives are oral histories which have been collected and analyzed in a particular way.

Typically, life history research aims to combine dimensions which have been separated out in other methodologies, for instance, the sociological, the ethnographic, and the historical (Bertaux, 1983), structure and agency (Elder, 1981), to produce a relational analysis of the *ensemble* of social relations (Ferrarotti, 1981), of the social *network* (DeCamargo, 1981). However, this emphasis on inclusivity, found, for example, in all of the articles in *Biography and Society* (Bertaux, 1981), should not distract us from the necessary selectivities which must also characterize all research.

Decisions must still be made concerning the relative emphasis to be placed on particular elements, the ways in which the elements are to be assembled for presentation, and the underlying set of assumptions within which the analysis is to be situated. Indeed, it is interesting to note that this relatively young research tradition has generated such remarkably diverse ways of framing life histories. While this method has been widely praised as a unique innovation, it still seems that theoretical, methodological and political presuppositions play crucial roles in different researchers' usage. In the field of education, for example, articles in Ball and Goodson's (1985) collection employ established developmental models to describe *Teachers' Lives and Careers.*

Other contemporary models for describing teachers' narratives include the creation of a fictive composite individual, in the work of Connell (1985), and the choice of exemplary individuals, in the work of Spencer (1986). I am uncomfortable with both these approaches. The first loses the integrity of the individual voice, while the second forfeits a sense of a social energy. Both seem to be pressing down very hard in the pattern-making process, and the results are too much like stereotypes.

Yet analysis is impossible without pattern-making of some sort. Using the work of both the Popular Memory Group and Bakhtin as theoretical justification for my own group biographies, I have tried to create more dynamic and dialogic patterns. Instead of reducing the diversity of women teachers to the single dimension of marital status (as is the case in Spencer) I have assembled groups of women with a number of connected self-identities in common. Instead of trying to explain social interaction by having one (male) university professor criticize the feminism of his pygmalion creation of an individual, albeit composite (woman) teacher, (as in the case of Connell) I have created a social space where the collective creators of a discourse can engage in a group conversation.

Text and Context

In Bakhtin's theory there are no isolated individuals, for the continual constitution and reconstitution of any worldview (in utterance) is inextricably bound up with its relationship to other worldviews, (in a system of intertextuality); all language is essentially social. "Each word," Bakhtin (1981: 293) says, "tastes of the context and contexts in which it has lived in its socially charged life," and,

> the living utterance, having taken meaning and shape at a particular historical moment in a socially specific environment, cannot fail to brush up against thousands of living dialogic threads, woven by socio-ideological consciousness around the given object of an utterance; it cannot fail to become an active participant in social dialogue (Bakhtin, p. 276).

Thus, unlike many other theorists, Bakhtin places primary emphasis on understanding texts within their specific and varied social contexts, for the "immediate social situation and the broader social mileau wholly determine—and determine from within, so to speak—the structure of an utterance" (Bakhtin in Clark and Holquist, p. 215).

The idea of group biographies which I have employed in my analysis is supported by a corollary of these points, that is, "no utterance in general can be attributed to the speaker exclusively; it is the product of the interactions of the interlocution, and broadly speaking, the product of the whole complex social situation in which it occurred" (Todorov, 1984: 30).

Thus, while apparently idiosyncratic and seemingly individual expressions can be observed in these narratives, the vocabulary which each woman has in common with other teachers in similar circumstances is considered to be more important for the purposes of this analysis. Bakhtin's notion of the *password*, "known only to those who belong to the same social horizon," (Todorov, p. 42) applies here, for important common verbal patterns do emerge within the narratives of each particular social group of teachers in particular social circumstances.

That this sense of a social "dialect" in Bakhtin (1981) corresponds not only to the Popular Memory Group's (1982) "general cultural repertoire," but also to West's (1982) "discourse," Gramsci's (1980) "collective subjective," and Fish's (1980) "interpretive community," is now plainly clear to me. But my application of this concept to my analysis of particular groups of teachers came slowly.

After dismissing all versions of individual analysis, I chose to study the narratives of Catholic nuns first, since they belonged to what seemed to be the most obviously articulated social group. With colored markers I coded what I called *personal, social,* and *work* relations, as well as any references to *religion*. But when I tried to write about these subjects separately, they seemed to be hopelessly entangled. My own analytic gestalt finally emerged only when I caught glimpses of a worldview, in the repetition of certain metaphors, and in frequent references to identity, meaning and death. I discuss this particular worldview in terms of a social language or discourse in Chapter Three of the book.

The social circumstances of other women were not so closely connected, and the assembly of a second group did require slightly more intervention. When I considered the narratives of some sixties activists, I began to see the ways in which they were connected to other secular Jewish women who were working in inner-city schools and had participated in projects of the Left. I discuss this discourse, and its preoccupation with work, in Chapter Four.

It was only after I had outlined the contours of each of these two discourses from the narratives that I begin to make connections to corresponding discourses in the philosophies of education (pragmatism and existentialism) and in the larger social world (Catholic and Marxist tradition). I found that I was less fluent in the cultural repertoire of the black women teachers, and that, in this case, I needed to move back and forth between analytical expositions of African-American vernacular and literary tradition, and the narratives themselves, before I could identify the constituent gestalts of slave narrative and signifying. I discuss this discourse in Chapter Five.

The narratives of these three groups of progressive teachers present an interesting set of contrasts. Placed side by side, they create a kind of Bakhtinian dialogue on the possibilities of alternative discourse; together they stand in opposition to dominant interpretations of the meaning of education.

The Significance of Ordinary Teachers' Voices

"Each word is a little arena for the clash of and criss-crossing of differently oriented social accents," says Bakhtin; "a word in the mouth of a particular individual is a product of the living interaction of social forces" (Bakhtin in Clark and Holquist, p. 220). I remember when I was conducting my own interviews being infuriated by an interview with a Harvard professor in *Education Week;* unfortunately, his dismissal of "plain old vanilla-ice-cream-type teachers" is just one of many examples of the long-standing denigration of women teachers by the dominant ideology. The words of ordinary teachers, loudly denying that kind of definition, need to be taken seriously in the academic world, and Bakhtin's theories suggest one way for that to begin.

The most important contribution of Bakhtin's theories, from my point of view, is the way in which they make possible the combination of a serious intellectual analysis of women teachers' narratives with a profound respect for their authors. I like to imagine Mikhail Bakhtin, himself an elementary school teacher and for many years "a beloved teacher" in a teachers' college (Holquist: xxv), smiling on a project which celebrates the words of ordinary teachers. The theories which he has articulated certainly encourage that notion.

> Dialogism is not intended to be merely another theory of literature or even another philosophy of language, but an account of relations between people and between persons and things that cuts across religious, political and aesthetic boundaries. Despite the enormous range of topics to which it is relevant, dialogism is not the usual abstract system of thought. Unlike other systems that claim such comprehensiveness, Bakhtin's system never loses sight of the nitty-gritty of everyday life, with all the awkwardness, confusion, and pain peculiar to the *hic et nunc,* but also with all the joy that only the immediacy of the here and now can bring.
>
> And unlike other philosophies that opposed radical individuality in the name of the greater primacy of socially organized groups, Bakhtin's philosophy never undercuts the dignity of persons. In fact, dialogism liberates precisely because we are all necessarily involved in the making of meaning. Insofar as we all involved in the architectonics of answerability for ourselves and thus for each other, we are all authors, creators of whatever order and sense our world can have (Clark and Holquist, p. 348).

3

An Existential Discourse of Catholic Women Religious Teachers Working for Social Change

Introduction

As the open-ended structure of the narratives allowed women to introduce subjects of major importance to them, I began to hear recurrent allusions to their religious upbringing or to their moral values and motivations.[8] Among my initial contacts, these themes appeared with more regularity than the overtly political explanations of their activism which I had expected. At one point I began to anticipate an opus entitled "Quakers, Catholics and Communists." That the communists never materialized is a subject I discuss elsewhere.

Having concluded that religion could not be ignored, I decided to allow myself more scope for investigating this new theme by adding another group to the study: women teachers whose whole lives appeared to be organized around religion, Catholic women religious (nuns). Thus I came through an indirect route to include representatives of a significant set of women teachers whose contributions have been particularly ridiculed, marginalized or ignored.[9]

More than the other individuals whom I interviewed, these women formed a coherent group.[10] The concrete network which joins Catholic women religious became evident from their initial recruitment. To have contact with one woman was to have potential access to all the women in her congregation, including those living a thousand miles away. The present high degree of intercongregational cooperation meant that I was referred to women from other religious orders as well. Every nun I met, including those who did not participate in the study, seem to know the "political" reputations of a large number of other nuns, whether they were acquainted with them personally or not.

Starting with one religious order, from which I interviewed three women in three different cities, I was referred to two other women, each belonging to a different congregation. A person whom I had contacted independently, in yet another city, proved during her narrative to be a former member of one of the orders to which I already had connections. Her narrative, as well as that of another nun, from a fourth congregation, also solicited independently, significantly echoed the life stories which I had heard from those women more directly connected to each other.

The network to which Catholic nuns belong could be explained in terms of institutional arrangements. In the historical period when the vast majority of American nuns were teachers, profession of vows most often meant joining the teaching profession. Convents were built beside, attached to, or sometimes even as a part of, school buildings. Nuns lived together with their colleagues. They participated in virtually identical activities, and came in day-to-day contact with the same small group of people: the women with whom they lived, the children whom they taught, and, more remotely, the Catholic families of these children, and the parish priests. Their own education and welfare were coordinated by the congregation-at-large, within the confines of a Catholic universe. Thus, personal, work, and social relations were articulated to an extraordinary degree on a structural level; and a community of belief was simply taken for granted.

Yet in the narratives themselves, three of which include explicitly historical passages, such structures are seen as only a temporary phase, and a partial (often negative) explanation, of life in a religious congregation. A great deal of the content of narratives of nuns is concerned with Catholic schools, religious congregations, and the church as a whole, since these constitute the major sets of relationships within which these women live their lives. But, as in all life stories, there are selectivities and emphases, and the particular details and their ordering, as well as the implicit and explicit understandings in which they are set, tell a tale much deeper than organizational analysis.

When women organize their life stories, as they have organized their lives, around religion, they use language in special ways. And, because the women in this study are also progressive political activists, they use a particular "dialect" of religious language. Furthermore, in combination with the aforementioned, they talk about themselves as teachers in a distinctive way.

It was initially with this group that I began to use the concept "discourse", a consistent system of controlling metaphors, notions, categories, and norms which develops and delimits its speakers' conceptions of personal, work, and social relations.[11] The meaning of "discourse" as a way of perceiving became dramatically clear to me in one narrative which I found especially puzzling. At first I could not grasp its underlying coherence. On the one hand, this woman spoke in deeply thoughtful and highly unconventional terms about changes in her own teaching philosophy. On the other hand, she became quite flustered and inarticulate when asked to describe change in the political arena, finally grasping at cliches. "Radicals," according to her definition, were "terrorists" who hijacked and bombed innocent people. Yet, a "diagnosis" of "false consciousness," with whatever extenuating circumstances I could imagine, did not seem adequate.

Some months after the original interview, I received a letter from this woman, describing abrupt political changes with passionate enthusiasm. The lens through which the political events were filtered, however, was profoundly religious, even while some of the vocabulary was unconventional:

> Well, they finally got rid of both the bastards. Could you believe that the Philipine people (also Haiti) would ever rise up and get rid of him? I just knew he was done for when I saw the priests and nuns marching on the palace and putting little wooden crosses on the barbed wire. The other day a whole group of people stopped the army tanks by kneeling in the street praying out loud. The drivers of the tanks absolutely refused to run over them. Cory (a woman yet!) was educated over on ——— Street where my friend ——— teaches at ———, and at Mount Saint Vincent.

She "saw" this political event because it involved people and symbolism which she understood. The event itself was "written" in a religious discourse which she could "read" by virtue of being a member of the Catholic clergy, a woman, a teacher and a friend. And, as a "reader" of these life history narratives, I needed, in turn, to identify the religious language in which they were "written" before I could recognize their distinctive political theorizing.

Existential Questions; Religious Answers

It is not surprising that the discourse of the women in this group has so many points of convergence, for its speakers have lived similar sorts of lives for periods ranging from twenty to forty-five years. To say that their personal, work, and social arrangements have been virtually identical, however, is not to imply that they have been static.

Not only do these women have a common experience of highly regimented communal life; they have also all participated in the radical reorganization of their religious orders. Not only do these women have a collective memory of parochial school teaching; every woman in this group has made a substantive career change. Not only are these women fluent in the traditional language of the Catholic church; together they have become active translators and transformers of its words.

I am tantalized by the idea of comparing life histories narrated by these same women some twenty years ago with those they created for this project. Of course, no such texts exist. Indeed, at times, there is a feeling in these narratives that everything is fresh and original, and everyone is full of energy. At the same time, there is also a curiously haunting tone, evoked, perhaps, by the tremendous risk-taking involved in all these changes, but also, it seems, by the enormity of the tasks involved in the new "social justice ministry."

These inflections resonate with existentialist themes of freedom and responsibility; so do the notions of personal authenticity and rejected tradition which echo throughout these narratives. An existential disposition pervades these life histories, one which is at every point combined with a religious perspective. Questions raised by an existential experience of nothingness are answered through the creation (and recreation) of religious identity, while existential encounters with death are resolved through the (continual) renewal of religious life.[12]

Defining the Self: The Nun

In the narratives of these Catholic nuns, answers to the existential question "Who am I?" flow from a religious matrix. One woman mentions several times that she was born in a house at the apex of a triangle with the parish convent and rectory. Another woman's life story starts with the sentence, "I was professed in 1964"; the beginning of her life as a nun is, from her perspective, the beginning of her life.

Not every nun's narrative explains her decision to become a nun;

but two that did, describe their apparently inexplicable choice in clearly existential terms. Both recount difficulties in schools taught by nuns, remember generally disliking the nuns they knew, and describe themselves as "not the type" to join the convent. So, having lived as nuns themselves for more than twenty and twenty-five years respectively, they feel a need to explain this puzzle in their stories. One woman tells of an existential crisis and a religious conversion:

> I think what happened was the year before that I was going
> through a kind of life crisis. Something about the meaning of
> my life. I suppose that this was probably an identity crisis. It
> seems like all my life I had had Catholic doctrine and stuff
> shoved into me and I can remember hating the stuff that I did
> in high school and when they talked about grace I always
> thought it was boring. I was more interested in sex.
>   I guess what happened was I really went through some kind
> of conversion. Things that I had formerly just laughed at or
> just had really never thought about except on a superficial level
> I started to take seriously. I think I really wanted to know
> what the meaning of life was, and what the meaning was for
> me, really, I guess. I decided, at that time, and I can remember
> deciding it so I know it was important to me. I decided that, if
> I had something to do with my life, something important, the
> thing I most wanted to do was to give it to God, and I think I
> thought that by going into the convent I could find God.

The search for meaning was not settled for all times by this decision; she continues to ask herself this question. Even last year, she recounts,

> I remember kneeling at mass in the morning and suddenly I
> had this very clear gut feeling that what I had done with my
> life was really good and important and that I still wanted to do
> it. So however muddled my reasons were then, I guess they still
> have a quality, have a clarity about them still and now I just
> think what I did was the right thing.

Being a nun is, furthermore, no guarantee of meaning, according to this narrative; although she herself finds authenticity in her construction of that role, this woman speaks critically of the possibility of becoming what she calls "canned nun."

For the other woman who unpredictably entered the convent, the title "nun" is, in Carol Christ's (1980) vocabulary, a "false naming," because it is used by those who seek to curtail her ministry to gay and lesbian Catholics. She sees the hurling of the epithet, "traitor" at a public meeting, together with the affixing of the label, "class clown," in her childhood days, as attacks on her authentic self. Although her original decision to join the convent "all of sudden, just seemed like the right thing," and living in her community still does, she is no longer comfortable with the name "Sister," because of the expectations some people attach to it.

> So, I more and more don't want this *Sister* thing. To be any-
> thing special or different or. . . . I get angry when people say
> "*Oh,* but you're a *nun!*" Right. "Well, you don't dress the way
> . . . you don't dress like a nun." Well that doesn't make any
> sense, because I am, and this is how I dress.

Subjected since childhood to experiences of nothingness in the form of destructive devaluations of her self, this woman was nevertheless able to maintain and nurture her authenticity. While her narrative recounts her positive experiences in teaching, contact with nature, friendship with "those who had no other friends," and small group community living, she does not attribute her sense of freedom to any particular source:

> So people call me names, so what? I don't really know how I
> got freed from that. Really, I don't. But I am, and it's a wonder-
> ful feeling. When people actually said, "This is the class
> clown," or "She's a troublemaker," I felt like . . . that was then
> who I was. You know, I don't like that, because I'm more than
> that. I'm bigger than that.

Defining the Self: The Teacher

The passage in which this woman describes entering the convent, to the surprise of "everyone," even to some extent herself, tells how her religious superiors had their doubts, "and, yet, they didn't tell me to leave." Without a pause, the next sentence continues, intensely, "I, all my life wanted to be a teacher. *All my life.*" Elsewhere she reiterates: "I'm a teacher at heart; I will always be a teacher." In her narrative, entering the convent is inextricably associated with becoming a teacher, and teaching takes on an existential quality in this connection and in the way she links it to nature.

Echoing Christ's analysis of nature as a place where women can make contact with the meaning and power withheld from them in society, the girl who was always in trouble in school found "the earth" to be one of "the most influential people," and "significant teachers" of her childhood: "I very much was raised, I believe, by the earth. I was very attentive to myself, as I was growing, and as I say, I learned a lot from the earth. I probably learned more from earth than I did from any teacher in school." And, indeed, although she described her own teaching philosophy and methods in thoughtful detail, she was unable to locate their source in any part of her teacher education or any "school of thought."

According to Christ, women are particularly vulnerable to the experience of nothingness because of their powerlessness in society, but this makes them better able to identify with other victims, and to become involved in their struggles. The main reason this woman became a teacher, for example, was because of her recognition of the powerlessness of "little people." She wanted to create something that she herself had never experienced in school: a space in which children's authenticity could flourish.

> I wanted to make education alive for kids. I wanted it to be
> real. I didn't want them to feel like they were apart from the in-
> stitution, or that they were separate from it. That somehow
> there was meaning there for them, that they *could* make a dif-
> ference. I never felt I could make a *difference,* because I was al-
> ways in trouble.

While she was a teacher, one of the children in her class confided in her his fears of being homosexual, and a fellow teacher who was a very close friend disclosed that he was gay. She began to realize the oppression of gay and lesbian people and, as she "was always for the underdog," she went to work for their cause.

Defining the Self: The Activist

This woman is a very reluctant activist. She does not like the word "political"; she is "intimidated" by government. She describes herself as a shy person who began her ministry as "a simple presence," and was forced to speak out because of the positions taken by local government and the church. Her public debut as a spokesperson was at a City Council meeting in support of gay organizations' right to hold meetings in the Chamber of Commerce building, an action which she recounts in existential terms: "All kinds of people were there. And I said very loudly, and bravely, 'Sister (her own name), member of the Sisters of (name of her religious order), of (name of city).' "

Another version of the formulation, "I/we are, therefore I/we speak, therefore I/we are" appears in relation to her giving of homilies at the blessing of commitment of two gay people; "I am saying I recognize this relationship," and "I am saying very loudly, yes, it does exist, and I affirm it."

The "new naming" by which the gay and lesbian Catholics tell "who *they* are," and "what is *really* going on in their lives," has fortified this woman's sense of who *she* is. The associations to which gay and lesbian Catholics belong are called "Dignity" and "Integrity"; and this woman feels "compelled" to be their chaplain, because she needs "to live authentically," "to find integrity" in herself. She has always spoken out against injustices, but now she is one voice within a newly defined community of voices. Membership in the new community shows her the falseness of the old institution. She has become deaf to what the church hierarchy is saying; it no longer "makes sense" to her. "I don't see the Pope as the Catholic church. The church is *these* people I am ministering to. They are the church, and they are saying from their life experiences who they are."

Yet the strength which she derives from her work with gay and lesbian Catholics goes beyond "group solidarity." The "prevailing problematic" of gay and lesbian rights has been, in the words of Cornel West (1982), "existentially appropriated." Her quest is rooted in the powers of being. Within the religious discourse of Prophetic Christianity, the final recourse for "the negation of what is" and "the transformation of prevailing realities" is the transcendent God, says West. In this woman's words, "Well, *maybe* I am a traitor to the Pope, and what he says, but I'm definitely not a traitor to the word of God. The reason I'm here, is because it is very clearly what I hear in the Scriptures."

Two nuns make a point of distinguishing between political action taken for religious motivations and that which is not. Speaking of the volunteers who work with her in a program for women in prison, one woman emphasizes:

Many of them don't come from a religious *motivation*. And I *do,* I *do,* because Jesus said "I've come to announce freedom to captives." And I know that they have been treated as less than equal in their education, housing, home, job preparation, employment, they've been treated as inferiors. I *know* that. And I feel that each of us have a responsibility to do what he/she can to balance the scales of justice.

The other woman, who now works with street people, makes a functional point about her perspective:

And, for me, I see a real difference when my motive and my expression of who I am and what I'm about comes from a belief in the gospel, rather than out of anger. What happens in my experience is that when people act out of anger they burn out quickly. But when people act out of gospel values, there's a better chance that they're also going to be in touch with. . . . When I came to an interview here, I was told, "If you see yourself as the one who has to do everything, you won't last. If you see yourself as part of the ministry of God's work, you will last. And you'll be one instrument that God can use to work."

This is expressive not only of a distinctive understanding of the process of political practice, but also of the role of the individual, of the nature of the goals, and of the location of ultimate power.

West (p. 96) echoes and expands upon these women's formulations in one of his summaries and defenses of the discourse of Prophetic Christianity:

The Christian project—even the Marxist-informed Christian project—is impotent in the sense that within the historical process, ultimate triumph eludes it and imperfect products plague it. *Yet, more important, there are varying degrees of imperfection and much historical space for human betterment.* For Christians, the dimension of impotency of all historical projects is not an excuse which justifies the status quo, but rather a check on Utopian aspirations which debilitate and demoralize those persons involved in negating and transforming the status quo. Ultimate triumph indeed depends on the almighty power of a transcendent God who proleptically acts in history but who also withholds the final, promised negation and transformation of history until an unknown future.

Of course, not every version of the Christian project is progressive, as West illustrates in his political typology of the varieties of religious discourse. Distinctions need to be made not just between Christian and non-Christian positions, but also within Christian discourse itself. In fact, the definition of what it means to be a Christian is a subject of ideological struggle.

The process of self-naming always takes place within the social context which is also a site of ideological struggle. The "new naming" of themselves by gay and lesbian Catholics has not been left unchallenged. The "false naming" of the gay rights activist by an opponent was an assault in an ideological battle, as was the attempted "un-naming" with which another activist was threatened.

This personally and politically assertive woman was not interested in the anonymity of the research project because, she told me, she would rather have her causes publicized through the use of her name. Throughout her narrative she explicitly announces her identities, ("I've been a nun for forty-five years"; "I have been a teacher more or less in some way or another for forty years"; "I am Jewish-Christian relations, and women"), and emphasizes their religious foundations ("So I feel that I do that which is God's will"). Probably for this very reason, her "naming" was being seriously threatened by the church hierarchy at the time of our meeting.

For a number of years she had been one of the leaders of several groups within the Catholic church which challenged the teachings of the hierarchy, particularly on subjects related to women in the church. In 1984, after some American bishops had made abortion a partisan issue, she signed her name, together with 96 other *Catholics for a Free Choice,* to an advertisement in The New York Times calling for a public dialogue on the issue.

The way in which this woman structures her narrative of these events is more important than the content which she communicates. Accounts of the episode can be found elsewhere, as it was, and still is being widely covered by the media. But in this account we can see several sets of assumptions which gave shape to the actions and understandings of the participants themselves.

Throughout the passage dealing with this issue, this woman speaks in the first person plural ("we signed it"); this was an action taken as a group. In emphasizing the importance of "sticking together," she is critical of the men who were originally part of the group, and who later "conformed." As men, she notes, they have the prospect of gender-exclusive promotion; as men, they do not have the experience of gender oppression, and of solidarity with "women who are in a hard corner."

Thus, her definition of the group is, in the last analysis, as women within the church struggling against the male hierarchy.

Gender is a primary issue in this woman's narrative. "My own cause is women," she reiterates throughout her story, and in one strikingly existential definition of her activism, she declares, "I am women." While she extends the circumference of her concern to include women throughout the world, specifically mentioning her own trips to India, Lebanon, and Latin and Central America, it is clearly women living in poverty for whom she works. And within this group, she has now focused on women in prison. At the same time that she has been shifting her energies to the specific cause of poor women, she has also been a primary organizer of her own cohort of women co-workers. She was a founder of a cross-congregational association of Catholic women religious, protesting their position in the church; she established the organization of interdenominational church women who work with women in prison; she has connections with the National Organization for Women. The public petition on abortion came out of a preexisting network of a particular group of Catholic women religious and their associates.

The process by which the church hierarchy aimed to "un-name" those who signed the petition was, it appears, to be conducted by remote control. Neither the individuals involved nor their assembly as a group were ever directly addressed by the church hierarchy. Instead the process of censure was initiated through the separate religious orders to which the members of the group belonged. But here also, it seems, the solidarity of the organizational group (of women) won out against a hierarchically imposed authority (of men). While this woman recounts other examples of individual members of her religious congregation criticizing her work, in this instance she emphasizes the fact that her religious superiors "stood by us, you know. And in effect, they said 'We can find no cause to dismiss so and so.' "

As the word "dialogue" suggests, this woman together with her co-signers took for granted the existence of distinct groups within the Catholic church. The call for "dialogue" also proposes interaction between groups of equal status. Any claim of the church hierarchy to exclusive or higher authority is dismissed ("They are always quoting themselves and each other to find authority. Find a better authority than that!"). Like the nun who was an advocate for gay and lesbian Catholics, this woman finds authority for her actions through the immanent voices of her constituency, women living in poverty, and, ultimately, in the transcendent power of God. The power of the hierarchy is radically undercut when its members are not seen as intermediaries to the greater power. Not only does this woman declare: "I didn't take vows to the Pope. My vows were made to God"; she has also joined a "noncanonical" community, so she will "always be a nun," even if the makers of the laws say she is not. The approval from the hierarchy which was previously understood as legitimating religious organizations is simply bypassed, and groups name themselves as communities dedicated to religious ends.

This woman does not rest her case only on the language of religious belief; she also speaks the language of social scientific analysis. That some of the hierarchy saw the letter as a confrontation with a small group of "minions," rather than a conversation within the whole Church, she proposes, is an indication of their lack of understanding of contemporary realities. Research by the National Opinion Research Center, she notes, "showed that only eleven percent of adult Catholic couples, *only eleven percent,* follow the church's teaching on the use of contraceptives." In a Gallup poll taken in July 1984, she also observes, "of adult Catholics called, 77% believed that abortion was permissible in some instances." For a particular group within the clergy to assert authoritarian power under these circumstances is, in her estimate, an inept miscalculation.

> When we signed it, we didn't think it was gonna be radical.
> Some man, some man in the church, some bishops we think,
> here in this country, did not realize what it was gonna do. Un-
> leashed all that energy. We were grateful. Cause it gave us an
> instrument to *tell* people how we thought. But *he* had no idea.
> He thought we'd just sink in, you know, conform. Well, the
> men did, but we didn't. And we don't intend to.

Thus, the ideological position articulated by those who signed the newspaper advertisement is grounded not only in the strong network of the signers themselves but also in the (unorganized) majority of the total membership.

Identities and Institutions

So far we have seen examples in which the individual's identity is created by and creates a group identity. But these groups do not correspond to the institutions within which the women live their lives.

Working on their political projects, their networks include alliances across religious congregations, and denominations, in coalition with "lay-" and "non-" Catholics, in solidarity with other occupations, and even with their "clients." Even while these women remain members of a particular institution, they are breaching its boundaries by virtue of their wider networks.

But the women's perception of their relationship to the institution of the church is very different from their understanding of their relationship to their own congregations as institutions. The word "institution" is, in fact, always used in a derogatory sense to describe bureaucratic and legalistic trends in church organization. In the early part of this century, one woman complains, bishops were only interested in building institutions. Hence, they "kept pressuring sisters for hospitals and schools," without "thinking in terms of the broader society and each one having an individual gift to do something. They were thinking in terms of big chunks of labor."

The contemporary institutional church is seen as a regressive organization dominated by a privileged male hierarchy who exacerbate tensions by exerting authoritarian control. Nuns are relegated to the powerless periphery. They feel alienated from the institution, and see it as an impediment to their authentic identities. In the words of one woman, "You have to keep an aesthetic distance; otherwise it's cruel on your psyche." Another reiterates: "I don't wanna say I didn't *respect* the institution, but I tried to keep it in perspective, you know, and I always felt separate from it. And yet a part of it but separate."

At the same time, the women's own religious congregations are becoming less "institutionalized." Their legalistic phase is seen as an aberration, caused in part, according to one woman's interpretation of her order's history, by "the war." "We were cut off from our origins across the ocean. We had continued to observe every single thing the way it was before, and they had evolved."

Since the Vatican II reforms, communities are creating, and being created by, more democratic participation. "It seems as though the rule is now something that we make through our experience," one woman states; another observes: "I can't do the institutional kind of living any more. I will never be able to again. This is ordinary living. I'm an ordinary person. I'm very person-oriented. And I can't deal well with big institutions."

The women's perceptions of their leaders are not antagonistic, even though there are several ironic comments on inappropriate assignments "they" made in the past.

And there I did teach English and journalism and creative writing, newspaper and all that stuff. About seven years. Which at the time was just a royal pain. 'Cause I really wanted to be in nursing. So I was euphemistically there as the school nurse. I think they thought maybe that would keep me happy. I don't know.

Yet descriptions of disagreement generally stress processes of consultation, negotiation, flexibility, tolerance, and the contemporary development of "co-responsibility." Other sisters are assumed to be in good faith. There is a strong underlying sense of a common project, of an authentic striving for the common good.

When tensions between an individual and the religious congregation do appear, they are often concerned with the individual's work identity. The one woman who left the convent gave as one of her major reasons her discomfiture with the subject and level (college political science) which she has been assigned to teach. Another woman's work history, as noted above, fluctuated between nursing (which was her own interest) and teaching English, depending on the vacancies which the order needed to fill.

Work loads and preservice training are also mentioned as areas which were particularly problematic in the past. While several nuns in this study were selected for further education before they began to teach, one woman's experience is more typical of the common practice thirty years ago:

I was educated in eight different colleges before I got my degree. At the end of my freshman year it became apparent that there were not enough teachers to fill this grade school that we had. And I was told that I was going to take one set of summer courses and go and teach. And so I said Ok. I was *scared*. I was so scared. I worked *really* hard, and I worried a lot about those kids, because I really loved them. But I, there was a lot I didn't know when I started teaching. On other hand, what we *did* have was a fine sense of solidarity. So it wasn't like I was entirely on my own. And then I went to school in summer. For fourteen years. It took me fourteen years to get my degree.

In spite of these tensions, the lives of women religious are so tightly interwoven with their communities that changes in identity and/or context are potentially very traumatic.[13] Two women recreate experi-

ences of existential isolation in their narratives by associating the process of change with an encounter with death.

One woman who reluctantly accepted her "re-naming" to a position
of leadership in her religious community connects that transition to
her escape from a fatal car accident. Her first official act as coordinator
was to organize funerals for two friends with whom she would have
been travelling had she not taken up her new job one week before. The
association of these two experiences in her narrative suggests that she
was mourning the loss of her earlier identity, at the same time as she
was feeling lonely and isolated by her new managerial role. It must
have seemed as though her life was saved so that she could make her
special contribution to the community. After she had organized the
structural transition which the congregation had mandated for itself
(a whole-scale transformation of group relationships and individual
identities) she left the (now obsolete) position of coordinator to return
to her former occupation and ordinary membership in the community.

Another woman's re-naming originated in her search for more meaningful work, and only indirectly in connection with her congregation.
She had chosen her "life's work" when she joined a religious order
dedicated to teaching, and had received professional training and certi-
fication in that area. But, after teaching for twenty years, and becoming
a highly skillful practitioner, she began to feel "hollow"; she had lost
her sense of purpose. Around this time, she relates, one of her colleagues
was killed in a car crash. It was not only the death of a fellow teacher
which shocked her; it was the interpretation of that loss by the school
administration which impinged on her own fragile identity.[14]

> I remember when this Brother who was a very nice man died
> and the principal stood up and said, "Well, we had a problem.
> I was away in Europe this summer and when I got back, I
> found out that he had died. Brother died, and we didn't have
> anybody to take his place, but fortunately, we were able to fill
> the gap." I was just appalled, you know. Like I finally said,
> that's all the administration want, you know, someone to fill
> the hole.

Her own doubts about the meaning of her occupation made her
susceptible to others' devaluation of it. Her work "wasn't really valued"; she was "just another cog in the wheel" in the eyes of six different
principals, who "never knew what had come before and cared less."
When she was transferred after seventeen years teaching in the same
school, she "left without even a plastic plaque with my name on it,"

43

symbolic, in her eyes, of the non-being accorded to her person. She subsequently laid her teacher identity to rest, and, with the support of another artist, she began to redefine herself as a painter. At the time of our meeting, she was still working out the integration of her new role within her community; this included the major practical project of finding employment, as there was no suitable position within the schools her congregation operates.

Like the accidental deaths with which they are associated, identity changes appear in these two stories as ruptures, which cause disorientation, isolation, and (at least temporarily) destruction, and against which meaning must be recreated. Two other narratives which include encounters with death present deliberately chosen constructions of identity and meaning through group action. Disjunctures are immediately transformed by the religious and political projects within whose contexts they appear.

The deaths which appear in the narrative of a woman who works with the homeless are neither natural nor accidental; they have social causes. Deaths from exposure of the homeless can be traced to real estate profiteering, and to the allocation of government resources for military purposes. Nuclear research, the building of battleships, and funding of insurgencies, each remove money from social services, and each is in itself a cause of death. "I choose life," this woman declares, in a deliberate reconstruction of the right-wing "pro-life" phrase:

> Trying to help people choose life. Politically that's where I am. Now, it's difficult because I'm not . . . I cannot classify myself in the group of people who call themselves pro-life. OK? I'm not in that group, because their idea of pro-life to me is very limited. You know, "Capital punishment is fine," things like that. And when I choose life, I choose life for all people in all dimensions. And it doesn't matter, who the person is or where they live.

One of this woman's religious-political projects is the prevention of socially caused deaths through public manifestations of their existence. Participating in a "lie-in" at a nuclear research facility, a "die-in" on a battleship, and a "sit-in" on the Nicaraguan-Honduran border, this woman has progressed from naming the destructive function of an ordinarily invisible facility, to acting the part of an already deceased victim, to placing herself in danger of death. In each case, she was personally and publicly constructing a religious and political discourse in concert with the groups of which she was a member. Theory and practice, ideology and action were united in her "experience of putting my *body* where I believed." Death was defined, and conquered, in a particular formulation; and leadership, defined as the collective taking of public initiative out of personal conviction, was accepted as an identity.

The moment of ideological victory over death is vividly described in this woman's account of her encounter with death on the Nicaraguan border. Ordinary fears are transcended as ideology put into practice becomes an empowering force, and the isolated individual is bonded with the group, and with the transcendent God:

And I remember saying to someone that, I studied a lot about grace, but being at the border when the soldiers lifted their rifles, it was a real powerful experience of grace. Because there was no other way!

Before I went to Nicaragua, like just a few days before, they had the helicopter incidents and everything, and I was saying, "Oh my God," I said, "I'm carrying a little American flag, and if we have problems, I'm gonna raise it and say 'I'm on your side!' " Everything I believe in goes down the drain when it comes to that. And I told people "Now, if someone tells me to raise my hands and they're gonna shoot me, I'll break every record in the race," I said, "I'll run so fast."

And I remember thinking that when I was at the border. I started to laugh to myself thinking, "God, all the things I said before I came here." And it was like, I just wanted to say, "Shoot me if you want. But you're not going to destroy what we believe in, the power of Christ is so much stronger than those bullets and everything else." And I thought I can't believe I'm really thinking this.

And we shared as a group afterwards, and everybody agreed. Everyone was really afraid. But that fear was overcome with courage and it was an experience of what we read in, you know, Paul, when he says about the power of the risen Christ is in you. It was a real, I mean, a power that was within, that gave me strength to stand there, that's the resurrection power. And so it was an experience of so much I've studied. Being there.

The idea of "dying for what I really believe in" is now associated in this woman's mind with a feeling of "peace within me." In another woman's narrative, expulsion from religious life is symbolically equated with death and, even while she was making organizational maneuvers to prevent this existential un-naming, she willingly accepted the possibility of "dying" for what she believes:

> My dossier is on their top desk in Rome. And I'm sure they want my head, but they won't dare. I don't think they'll dare. If they do, I'll go. OK, I'll go. I've been a nun for forty-five years. I've been a faithful nun. But, OK, I'll go. It's a good cause to die for. *To stand with women.*

The Construction of the Consistent Self

It was the public manifestation of a particular religious and political stand in a full-page national newspaper advertisement signed by this woman and her cohorts which put her in jeopardy of her identity as a nun, threatening her existence within the church. But it is the continuous composition and publication of her ideas (in "over two hundred articles and several books") which contributes to her identity as an activist, giving her other grounds to say "I am."

While I was recording her narrative, she would pause from time to time to find me reprints from national magazines of other interviews she had given, and to show me relevant quotations. I later heard other members of her cohort use the same or similar phrases in their own media presentations about the newspaper advertisement, attesting to the way in which her statements grow out of her political connections, and more often take the form of "we are" than of "I am."

Her publications are contributions to the discourse of the networks to which she is attached; but her writings have also helped her explain her own life to herself. Faced with existential dread after the death of her parents, she was able to assuage her grief by interpreting the meaning of their lives in terms of their influence on her. Many of her acquaintances say they do not know the source of their activism, she observes; she traces her own back to her parents.

> I have been reflecting deeply about my childhood. And after my parents died, I couldn't talk about it. I was in such grief. We all were. But I wrote a chapter for a book, and that was a kind of release for me. And after that I could think more about my parents. 'Cause I was so in grief over their loss. It was a natural death at a natural time, but it was . . . and after that then I

began thinking. I wrote three chapters for different books on that subject. And, I think it's my parents. I definitely think so.

Well, my father and mother were very, very loving and caring. They were the town physician and the nurse. And the two of them took care of migrants, and they took care of everybody, of course, but they were very solicitous. Always. Yes, I think I got it from them. As I look back now, I think I can see the roots there in my parents. For example, I'm sure there was no Jew in our town. And yet my father, who was a very humble, simple, marvelous man, I can remember him saying, "As we treat the Jews, so God will treat us. And as a country treats its Jews, so God will treat them." And I didn't think much about it. But as I look back, I think that made a *deep* impression on me, and I think it's true.

Political sociology has investigated the relationship between childhood experiences and political socialization; and it has analyzed the influence of parents on their children's political formation. What is important about this passage is that the speaker, a former political science professor, makes such a connection in her own life. She is asking an existential question: "What was the meaning of my parents' lives?" and, she has constructed a religious-political-sociological answer: "They made me an activist."

In another section of her narrative this woman rejects the suggestion that she was ever not an activist, declaring: "I am consistent; I am very consistent." In the passage above she constructs a narrative consistency which stretches over time, interpreting the past (her childhood) in relationship to the present (her parents' death), and ranges across spheres bonding together personal, work and political relations (the intergenerational reproduction of professional care for needy clients). Political action is explained in an ethical vocabulary of love, care and solicitude, for, always at the center of this consistency, organizing all its dimensions, is religion.

The Language of Relationship

A particular normative vocabulary is threaded through all the narratives in this group, and binds together the personal, work and political relations of all its speakers. Moral imperatives are explicitly evoked throughout the narratives, and they are interwoven with a system of metaphoric representations of *what ought to be.*

One woman's explanation of the consistency and complexity of her moral identity makes use of several different kinds of metaphors. Calling herself an "existential phenomenologist," she uses vocabulary from her academic studies in that area: "My identity as a Sister of ——— is the primary focus of my identity, you know. Within that identity, I play lots of roles. But that's, in existential jargon, that's my primary 'projet.' " But she also chooses to explain her self through such symbolic forms as a triangle, a circle, an infinity sign, and a lazy Susan.

The triangle and the circle are configurations of the religious context within which this woman sees her self-formation. The house in which she was born becomes an analog for herself as she describes its position in relationship to the Catholic parish buildings:

> What I learned as a child, growing up in my house, was rein-
> forced in the church and its position in our lives, and while I
> joke about living in that triangle between the convent and the
> rectory, I also know that we grew up knowing priests and sis-
> ters as people. Not some kind of magic things.

When she tells of an early teaching assignment in that parish and a later return to live in the same neighborhood, she describes the feeling of "coming full circle." Using yet another geometric symbol of unity and integration, and moving her hand to draw a figure eight as she speaks, she reiterates her interpretation of the process by which she has come to be: "And my own experience just reinforces that, so that I feel kind of like that infinity sign, that the church has reinforced my identity as a person and my person has been reinforced by the values and symbols and the rituals and the culture of the church."

"Body language" also reinforces this woman's explication of her identity when, expanding the symbolic mode, she holds up one hand, and points to her palm with a finger of the other hand, saying, "There is this identity. And there is this lazy Susan on which the roles are." Then pointing to each finger she lists such roles as working and praying, emphasizing the way in which they are "infused," so that, for example, "my work *is* my identity. I am my work."

While some of this woman's metaphors are her idiomatic construc-
tions, she shares others with the larger group, specifically those of family and home. At first glance, there seems to be an irony to discovering these stereotypical female images in the discourse of progres-

sive political activists, who, additionally, have lived their adult lives in the antithesis of a "housewife" role. Further examination, however, will show a particularly interesting reconstruction of the symbolism of these images.

References to families recur throughout these narratives. Sometimes the focus is on families of biological origin[15]; that conventionally defined grouping is even presented as a social unit which reproduces a particular moral discourse. Family appears in the narrative context together with childhood, religious community, school, church and state; its meaning is elaborated and developed in relationship to them, finally emerging as the embodiment of what ought to be, as a model for the transformation of those social relations which do not correspond to the speakers' moral discourse.

The Childhood Family

With the family, as with other topics, the internal organization of a life history does not often follow a neat, sequential chronology, but places emphases according to the significations of the speaker. One woman's narrative omits the period of her childhood, and hence, the role her family of origin played in those years; two other women mention these aspects of their lives only briefly. While some narratives describe the families of their childhood in glowing terms, not all the women see their original families as matching their ideal.

One woman describes a childhood experience of existential meaninglessness caused by her mother's schizophrenia.

It *really* caused havoc in our family. And, since I was the youngest, and the one at home, I was the only one still in grade school, I got a lot of the bewilderment. And I was just becoming . . . I was passing from sixth grade into seventh when the worst happened. The worst being that she decided that the communists were after us and that was why her marriage was unhappy, and why my father drank, and why. . . . Which was all crazy. And we had one of the large radio consoles with the luminous dial, and she thought the announcers could see into our home. And that they were manipulating her, and so on.

The first year. . . . It was really miserable. My whole seventh grade. She was very unpredictable. I took piano lessons and she was the one who had started me, and she would come and slap

my hands at the piano and tell me not to play that *wicked* music. And I was playing *Brahms,* you know! I'd cry, and I'd say
"I have to learn this! My teacher gave me this to learn." Oh,
once I remember she hit me over the back with a butcher knife,
and . . . some things like that happened that were really kind of
bizarre. And made it very scary.

When her mother was committed to a mental institution, she was sent
to a Catholic girls' boarding school. She never returned home; she
joined the convent directly out of high school.

Denied access to meaning in her fragmented family, she was able to
escape her mother's idiosyncratic discourse in a community of understanding "sisters." As she was still a child, and, in her own phrase,
"just becoming," her identity was created within this surrogate family.

When I entered, I pretty well told my family I didn't need them
any more. I had learned to love and respect the people I had
gone to school with, and I really did love the sisters. I had
some real young, good, intelligent teachers. Who are still my
best friends. They're like five years older than I am. And I really admired what they taught me, and I wanted to . . . I was al-
truistic. I wanted to do something for somebody else, but I really needed a family. So I got them both!

From this woman's perspective, the religious community is characterized by an inclusivity which surpasses that of the family of biological
origin. She notes, for example, that counted among the sisters in her
congregation

is a woman whom we raised from age three, who was left as a
child with the sisters in our order by her father who didn't
want her. Cause she was too sick. And we raised her, and she
grew up, she worked in the kitchen. She visited her father very
often. She's now seventy-five, and lives in ———, with us
still. Her parents have been dead a long time. And she was as
much a member of our order except that she was not mentally
real capable.

The religious community, not the family of biological origin, was the
childhood family for these two women, providing them with moral
and material support in their formative years.

Religious Community as Family

The number of times the name "Sister" is used in these narratives would be striking to an uninitiated reader. Of course, historically, the Catholic Church has used the language of kinship to describe relationships among its members, and so such terms are part of the taken-for-granted vocabulary of the narrators. In fact, the use of "Sister" has somewhat declined among Catholic women religious in recent years, and this was evident in some narratives. But, I would like to suggest, it has been discarded for parallel reasons to the simultaneous dismissal among some other women of the titles "Mrs." and "Miss": to evade the aspects of "false naming" with which it had become associated, and to signify less formal and more personal relationships.

However they may be phrased, constituent familial relationships remain a central focus of the narratives. Whereas "sisterhood" is not the newly constructed, self-conscious naming of the contemporary women's movement, it consistently appears as a consciously valued and deliberately reproduced relationship. So, for example, one woman tells how she came to appreciate her relationships with friends in the convent; when one of them was posted elsewhere, and later left the order, "I went through a terrible kind of loss. It was as though I had lost a member of my family. Like we were really close."

Sharing is presented as the essence of sisterhood, in its moments of personal delight: "I mean, just sitting down and sharing a cup of coffee with your sister, I mean, that is a unique gift," and in its ordering of group relations,

And, if there's anything religious people, religious women have really experienced, it's community. How *all kinds* of us from all different attitudes and walks come together, and we make a home for each other. We have some sisters in our order, I thought, "How the hell did they ever get here!" I mean *come on!* But they were part of us. And we included them.

This sharing is not based on such standards of merit as intelligence. An assumption of human equality makes this family compassionate; they learn to "feel *with*" others, rather than to pity from a superior position.

We have one little sister who was under four feet. When you heard her speak, it was really sad. The rest of her family was real intelligent. She was somewhat retarded. She spoke . . . she would say something three or four times, and usually in the same, exact same sentences. . . . She was a *good*-hearted little person. Worked real hard, did what she was told, cried a lot. But she wasn't of an intellectual caliber that she could ever feel like she belonged. Except that what she did, is she did belong, because she contributed to the work. It was good for the rest of us, because we learned.

We learned compassion. We learned, compassion is not pity. Compassion is solidarity with people. Based on the fact that we're both people. Without any other conditions. It's standing with people in their suffering or in whatever, you know. And that's good, you have to learn that. It took me a long time before I had any compassion for that person, cause she was such an *annoying* person. She'd come and talk to you and say things over, three and four times when you were trying to get something done, she would come and talk to you. But little ——— was an asset to our community. When she died, we felt bad.

School Community as Family

In these narratives, the norms associated with the religious congregation as family are extended into other spheres of social relations; these women have the same moral expectations in the work arena as they do for their personal relationships. The emblematic tale of the retarded child taken in by the religious congregation is echoed in this same narrator's story of her handicapped student.

One of the things that I always try to do is look out for the ones that were on the frazzled edge of it. My first year teaching, I had ———. I don't know where ——— is now, and I hope you don't print his name. Ok, but ——— had a clubfoot. He was a third-grader who was maybe two inches taller than anybody else in the grade, because he had failed once. He was a little towhead with a crew cut, with a little toothy grin, skinny little kid, and always went as fast as he could on his little clubfoot.

I remember the highlight of my first awful year as a teacher was that ——— turned to me and said, "You're the best teacher I *ever* had!" In all of his three years of school, *four* years of school, in third grade! Eh! I was *so pleased*. But I think that kind of kid always attracted me because . . . I knew what it was like.

Having known the existential nothingness of being on "the frazzled edge" of her fragmented family of origin, this woman feels at one with other lost children, and is moved to connect them, as she herself was drawn in, to a new family. And, in the reciprocal arrangement of her narrative, the givers of the gift of inclusion are themselves rewarded by acceptance, reinforcing her theme that "there's a reason everybody is included."

Coming from the same root as *com*passion, the word *com*munity is also used in these narratives, and family is frequently presented as its embodiment. Both in its conventional usage (as in reference to the "religious community,") and in its more deliberately defined examples, this characterization of family accentuates the congruence of the members of the group.

Using such a pattern of association, another woman contrasts two different schools in which she taught. In the one which matched her expectations, she says, "I remember we worked really hard on establishing faith community in the school, and when I was leaving there people told me that the administrative team really did model to the school what faith community was about." She chose to leave the other school because she thought it destroyed the equality and authenticity which she considered qualities of a family environment; in its embodiment of violent hierarchical authority (which, we must note, is a competing definition of family) it seemed to her more like a prison.

And the reason I left was that I didn't agree with a lot of the philosophy in the school. I really believe that a school is a place where people come together, and form some kind of a community, and it's *not* a prison, and if it's likened to anything it's likened to a family rather than a prison. And, my experience in that school was that it was *much* closer to a prison. And I was not into prison ministry at the time!

So I decided, I will get out of here. And I just didn't like the way the young men and women were being treated. I didn't think it was practicing what I believe in. I believe in authority, but I believe in nonviolent authority. And there's such a thing that we each have our own authorship, and we speak out of that.

And I think teenagers in high school, have authority that's rightfully given to them by God, and teachers need to listen to them. And in that school, it was . . . *We are the faculty.* I mean, one day it was actually announced over the PA, you will smile at your teachers. I mean, it was *really* . . . that was the day I said I need to get out of here. And there were just too many games being played.

The school community which is a family is characterized by relationships of love among its members. In one narrative, this love is defined in terms of enthusiasm, close personal ties, and positive encouragement:

Well, when I taught the first twenty years I loved the people I taught. I found great enthusiasm in myself and in them. I must say that I could name any student I ever had, both boys and girls, and, for each one I think I could name the five virtues that are outstanding in that person. And I think that's the essence of true teaching. To get to love your students, and then to use their virtues in order to bring them forward. Pointing out their virtues only, their faults only through their virtues. To them. The goal is to have the child feel at home. And love school. And run to school.

Another woman creates a narrative parallel between her feelings towards members of her religious congregation and her relationship with her students. In an almost identical construction to one quoted above ("I had learned to love and respect the people I had gone to school with, and I really did love the sisters"), she explains her decision to join the convent in terms of love:

And I got very close to the sisters there. Was very close to the sisters of ———. Anyway, because they were the nuns who taught in the schools. And I loved them dearly, although I didn't like some of them personally, I loved them as a whole. I loved the sisters of ———. I loved their spirit.

And, she uses the same vocabulary to describe her affinity for the adults and children with whom she worked in schools: "We worked with marvelous people. People whom I still correspond with today, and I love dearly. I had a junior homeroom, and I *loved* juniors. So much more than any other group in high school. Juniors are really *neat* kids. They are a lovely bunch of kids."

Church as Family

The love described in connection with the religious congregation and the school community is neither that of spouses nor of parents and children, two possible familial versions of that emotion. Rather, it comes closest to love among siblings, so often called "brotherly" (*sic*) love, and historically known in Christian symbolism as "agape." The alternative set of church symbols in which the loving parent exercises benevolent power over the children is explicitly rejected as an acceptable relationship for the religious congregation, for the school and for the church itself.

Criticisms of the "Holy Father" occur frequently throughout the narratives. One woman calls him a "macho monster." But the rejection of the male parent's role in the family which is the Church goes deeper than problems with a specific person. Words etymologically derived from the paternal metaphor are used only in the derogatory versions of their definition. The pontiff and his associates "pontificate," using their position of leadership in a pompous and dogmatic manner. The protective and supportive meanings of "patronage" are lost, for its condescending aspects are more evident:

> And see I don't, I, I think I don't, I don't wanna destroy the whole system. You know, and I don't wanna say, it's no good. But I want to say, we're missing something. You know, we could be *so* much better . . . if we listen to people. If we *really* welcomed people, not patronized people, but I would like to see us be able to, us, the Catholic Church, strip the layers away, so that you're not afraid. I *feel* like we're very afraid to invite all kinds of people, into our embrace.

In these narratives, the true embrace, a gesture of love, is impossible for the male clergy, "who set themselves up and apart."

The Family Expanded

Across the narratives, the family of biological origins, the religious community, the school and the church are each in turn evaluated according to the criterion of inclusion. In certain narratives, the state, and the political, social and economic relations of the society at large are also judged according to the same demand.

The moral imperative "to invite all kinds of people" is repeated in several similar formulations in these narratives, for instance, "everyone's included at the banquet," "there is a reason why everyone is included," and in an explicitly familial vocabulary,

> I choose life for all people in all dimensions, and it doesn't matter who the person is or where they live. You know, there were no boundaries in my idea of . . . The world *is* my sister and my brother. It doesn't matter if you live in a certain street, or in a certain country. And, when I think of politics I guess, my stand is, whatever is for life.

The "human family" is the frame of reference for another woman; her commitment to the Jewish people is based on their "great gift" to that family: keeping "alive the idea of one God on this planet." The same woman praises the comprehensive composition of a particular political group because its board members are "from all over the country," "both academicians" and "grass-root workers who work with the poor"; "it's a beautiful coming together."

Particularly important manifestations of the ideals of inclusivity and reciprocity are the several passages which stress the cross-class basis for the moral-political project. Combining the previously mentioned motifs of family, love and support, one woman asserts a theory of class incorporation, even while noting its impediments:

> My sisters are married and they're all middle class and they love and support me and I love them. And I'm not throwing out the middle class. I'm not being foolish. Because I know that it's from the middle class that I came, and I know that we must move the middle class in such a way that they will incorporate the poor. See, the middle-middle, the upper-lower, if only the middle class could absorb the upper-lower, and maybe even the middle-lower. What's happening now is that, the lower-middle class is now becoming the upper-lower. That's a problem. And of course the yuppies have nothing in sight but they wanna become lower-upper.

This analysis is echoed by another woman who constructs a parallel between the history of her religious congregation and contemporary politics. The person who founded the order

56

was outspoken. He was kind, but he was outspoken and he believed in standing up for social change that was needed. And,
people who had money, it was their job to make the town
work. I was so excited the other day I saw in the paper that
the Democratic Party is beginning to speak again about the
common good. Horray, for the Democratic Party! And that
was very much the philosophy under which (he) operated. That
the common good depended upon those who had the money,
and could create the conditions for it. We all were responsible
for the common good in some way. Nobody was off the hook.
None of this, "I've got money and I can go do what I wanna
do." But they didn't have huge cities. It was so easy to tell
what a person was doing with his time and money. And so
easy to be pulled back in.

Again, certain impediments are acknowledged, but community, cooperation and the common good are set forth as ideal.

Service was the keynote of the Catholic school program in which
one woman approvingly participated; the project was organized to
produce (and reproduce) a cross-class and interracial perspective
among the participating students.

It was the coming together of all different schools, within the
religion program. And we had fifteen students from each
school, and they would be matched, an inner-city school with a
suburban, very wealthy school. Like we were matched
with ———— Country Day School. Their tuition's like . . .
Then it was $3,400.
But our kids and their kids would be in groups, doing some
kind of service. They might go to a nursing home, a day-care
center, a hospital. They'd do it as a group, they would be going
in the same places.
But what would happen is, one day a month, they would go
together, and one day a month there would be a reflection after-
noon. Talking about their experiences. What would happen in
that is the kids would learn about each other, and talk about
who *they* were. And kids from ———— would hear some of
the problems that kids from ———— had. And kids there
would hear some of the problems that kids at ———— had.
And what happened was, that they realized that, they came
from different backgrounds but they were all kids and they all
had different kinds of problems.

And they started looking at each other as people, rather than groups or classes of people. And that was, part of the purpose was that people could work together and they're still doing that. And that was a way of trying to get all different cultures together. And that worked really well.

Of course, these women are particularly connected to specific members of this vast human family, but they explain these attachments in terms of inclusion, rather than exclusion. One woman, for example, was accused of neglecting her "own people" while attending to the needs of others, but she did not accept the racial and religious boundaries which had been drawn by her critic.

Huh! You know that during the sixties my work for interracial justice was considered *very* controversial. Well, it was terrible, one of the nuns said to me, "Well, are blacks Catholic?" And I said "Only two percent." She said, "Well, then when you gonna work for us?" I mean, eh!

The breadth of her definition of a "people" was further demonstrated when, in the course of our conversation, the bombing of the (black) MOVE headquarters in Philadelphia the previous week was discussed, and this (white) woman remonstrated: "But you don't drop a bomb on one of your . . . I mean we're dropping bombs on *our own people.*"

Several women use a metaphor of oral-auditory communication to describe their state of receptivity to the needs of particular groups. The "vocation," "the call to service," is of course a long-standing Christian symbol, especially with reference to joining a religious community. Using, and transforming, this religious notion, one woman explains her "choice" of political projects in terms of her "listening heart:"

So I basically I see *all* of those issues as life issues. And I see them all as um . . . very pertinent to my whole life-style, because I've publicly professed obedience. And to me obedience is a listening heart. If I'm going to be faithful to my vow of obedience, it doesn't just mean in my community. It means that I'm going to be faithful to listening to what God is saying, in the realities of life. And then I have no choice . . . to be out there, you know, protesting the embargo. It's not a choice. I've made the choice . . . to be faithful to the gospel, and . . . as a religious I took a vow of obedience. And whether I was a religious or not, to me, it's faithful to my baptismal promises. But, as a religious I said *publicly* I will profess these. Well then I need to do it publicly. And I need to . . . whatever's *public* at that moment.

Another woman echoes the idea that one has only to listen to the contemporary debates to know what God is saying: "The motto of our founder was 'The will of the times is the need of God.' "

One woman describes the beginning of her connection to a particular group as a literal "call to service"; she was "hailed" and "petitioned" by the inmates in a prison which she was visiting.

Well, what happened, we've been going down to ———— for about seven years. What happened is that I gave a talk in ————, and one of the women there was one of the chaplains, and she said "Would you like to see ———— prison?" I said indeed I would, because ———— is a famous prison. Infamous prison.

So I went out there and, when I went through the women's division, the women came out of their cells, and they said "Now, can you read this and what do you think?" And it would be a brief. That they had written. And I said, "Well, I'm not a lawyer, but I do have friends who are lawyers." And then somebody else would bring you something. "Well, now, look, do you see my art?" And, "Would you look at it?" I'd say, "Well, I'm not an artist, but I have some *friends* who are artists," you know, and so . . . that's how we began having weekends down in ————.

Now we have a full-time women's advocate down there, serving the women full time. And she has organized groups of volunteers, thirty women. Through various churches in area.

Yet there must be a correspondence between the "listening heart" and the "interpellating[16] voice" in order for the message to be heard. This is not always clearly spelled out in the narratives. When there seems to be a perfect "fit" between ideology and practice, the appropriateness of one's actions is taken for granted.

To me it's just well this, this is life, this is everyday, so why is it radical? In fact, the first time I was arrested for civil disobedience, I didn't call up the provincial council to tell them. And I remember saying to someone, I remember saying, "Well, why, why should I call them? Isn't that a part of who I am? Isn't that a part of life?" And someone said to me, "Yeah, but it's not a part of everybody else's life!" And I understand their reason and I've called ever since.

Most often, there is no visible external source of interpellation; one is called by a voice within one's self. Sometimes this voice is explained as the voice of God; sometimes women just speak in terms of "doing what had to be done," of decisions which "just seem to be the right thing." One woman explicitly rejects voices of external persuasion in connection with religious vocations:

The other part-time job that I've had was in vocational, you know, congregation, so I was like an army recruiter. And that just wasn't my thing . . . 'cause I just . . . *believe* that if, if people have a vocation for a religious life, we don't have to go looking for them. They will come. They will want to be part of us. Um, and I will support, you know, women who come and who *want* to, you know . . . and encourage . . . but . . . it just didn't fit me.

The feeling of "fit" between ideology and practice is also expressed in terms of celebratory moments and rituals. One woman's master of fine arts project was a set of photographs which celebrated the life of her religious community. She describes the emblematic significance of one of these pictures:

The photos are all of our sisters. Some of them are up close, some of them, I have a great one that I used for the flyer for the show. And it's, uh, there are three people in the room. One is a woman whom we raised from age three . . . And she was as much a member of our order except that she was not mentally real capable . . .

So one was a picture of her with this friend of mine, and an older sister, and they were, they were kind of dancing, in the room. They just, the three of them. It's *wonderful* picture, I've got this sister with a hat on, with her arms out like this, and a *big* smile, looking right at the camera with an apron on. And I remember my photography teacher saying, "*These pictures! You never see pictures like this of nuns!*" And I said, "Yeah, yeah, I know you don't. *You aren't there when they happen.*"

The moment of dancing is spontaneous rejoicing; other celebrations are planned rituals. In the shelter for homeless women, the weekly sharing of a family meal embodies and celebrates the values of community:

> Well, Wednesday night is our community night. We have liturgy, and the women come to liturgy, liturgy twice a week. The women come. And Wednesday night we have supper up here, it's the only night we eat together as a community. But it's almost like a sacred night. No one plans anything on a Wednesday night. And we really choose to be with one another and share a lot of values and, just . . . I'd say prayer life in this house really does support the ministry.

Habitus

Another way in which these women express their ideological dispositions (their "habitus"[17]) is through metaphorical descriptions of the terrain upon which they see themselves situated. Physical features only appear on the ideological map when the habituée perceives a particular set of social relationships in that space. On a basic level, nuns are more likely to describe a local area as a "parish" than as a "neighborhood," or a "ward." In the more elaborate pattern of association in these narratives, the symbolism of the human-built landscape is consistently used to embody issues associated with change and problems connected with structure.

Self as Building

In a fundamental exploration of the dilemmas of change, one woman pictures the outmoded structures of her own personality in terms of a building.

> I remember I was just really stuck and I knew that I was going to take another whole step . . . I could feel it but I just couldn't get over the barrier. It was as though it was like a block, you know, like the former . . . door was closed and the other door

wasn't opened and I was stuck in a vestibule some place in between.

The resolution is also expressed using an architectural metaphor. The building which is the self stands, but her positioning and perspective within it changes. As she paints, she begins to feel more free to be an artist.

> And it was funny around that time I had, she had some pictures that her mother had taken when she was in Portugal and one of them was an open window. I must have done that open window in three different media. I really painted it in a lot of different ways. Tried some different things and I think it was an important time for me and I think what happened was when I did that I opened windows. In my own life. And I knew it was going to create changes and things were going to come from it and what happened was that I kept demanding more free time.

The Community as a Building

In the architectural metaphors used throughout these narratives, the habitus is not a permanent structure, but an ongoing construction process. Religious communities are criticized because, during their static phases, their structures operated as constraints and restrictions, like frames or boxes. One woman explains:

> See when we were in the, the first twenty years, we were kinda locked into a frame. And, it was very . . . very unusual to move out of that frame. I think I was one of the first in our whole community. But I did it simply because I went to an education department, and it was a national Catholic, but it wasn't run by the church. It wasn't official Church organization. But I think maybe my leadership did think so. I don't know. I myself hadn't even thought of it at the time.

Another echoes:

> I couldn't stand it! They were so straight-laced. And the expectations were, the three I was living with, there was one who

was just a honey, the other two were like . . . and I could not *stand* it! Here I am an artist you know and into . . . alternative life-style stuff, and . . . it's probably why I joined the convent to begin with, being alternative to what I had . . . Trying to always find something better, and they were *so* straight-laced, and boxed in, and I just couldn't stand it.

The communities continue to stand, but, like the building mentioned above, they have been subjected to drastic renovations due to the dramatic changes in the perspectives of the inhabitants.

As the clothing previously worn by nuns was known as a habit, discussion of its meaning is pertinent to an understanding of habitus. In its day, the habit was not necessarily an incumbrance, according to one woman who recalls: "I marched in Selma in full habit. The James Meredith march through Mississippi in full habit." Yet, over time, according to other narratives, it lost its meaning, and became a "habit" in its negative sense, that is, "a tendency to act in a particular way, acquired by frequent repetition of the same act until it becomes almost or quite involuntary." (O.E.D.)

Oh, heavens. It's got, being a sister is, has to do with your attitude, it has nothing to do with, what street you live on and what clothes you wear. It doesn't. It has *nothing* to do with that. It makes me *angry* when people say about the habit, you know. It has nothing to do with it! If you can't tell that I am a sister by my commitment or my attitude, then forget it.

Women as Builders and Demolition Workers

These women are not content to live in outmoded habits, nor in a structure that someone else built. Sometimes they portray themselves as builders. In her discussion of the issues involved in a reproductive freedom campaign, one nun describes both the potential of the women with whom she works, and the need for change in the church, in architectural terms: "A woman had to be . . . she had to be the architect of her own body. She had to make her decisions. And then she would be willing to *live* by her decisions, if she could make 'em; The hardest thing was abortion, and the right of a woman to make her own decision, just because I knew it was a threshold in the church, beyond which . . . but you see it already *is* a consensus."

I Answer With My Life

Sometimes these women envision themselves as part of a demolition crew. Prisons are presented in these narratives as the epitome of repressive structures, and one woman recalls a moment of religious liberation within such a context using architectural terms:

> The last time we were there, I went to a huge gym. and that
> was gonna be the worship for the men. And . . . this woman, a
> Presbyterian minister, the woman was leading them, in prayer,
> in song, and they practically took the roof off that gym singing
> the sacred hymns. And I thought, that's wonderful. Yes it is, in,
> in a woman.

The Building as the Home

The positive aspects of structure, the healthy components of the habitus, are portrayed in terms of the home. When the social landscape is viewed through the lens of moral expectations, not every collection of people living together is a family, and not every common dwelling-place is a home. Childhood dwellings are not necessarily homes; neither are convents.

Several women make distinctions among the different convents in which they have lived. Comparing two of her early postings, one woman sees the emotional atmosphere of each community embodied in its physical arrangements. In the first situation, "the place was really bare . . . just a bed and a chest of drawers"; then she was sent to a convent where "I was allowed to pick out my own bedroom and I don't know . . . the room was nice and there were so many things about it that I really liked. There was a chair, there was a desk, there was a built-in closet. . . ."

In the first instance, the buildings and the community itself were large, established structures; the second convent and its connected school was brand new, "and it was as though we were making *our* dent on it, our impression, and it was an easy way to start (teaching) in high school too because there weren't any traditions." So, as she was young and energetic herself, she was glad to move from the first situation to the new convent and school: "By the time I went on to ——— I was just really glad to go. I shook the dust of ——— off my feet and moved. Jeez, there were just so many things I hated about that that I left behind me. Awful. Anyway, I got to ———. And I felt like I had come home." Beside having a correspondence between her

64

own and the community values, and an appropriate embodiment of those values, this woman needed to be an active maker of the structure within which she lived in order to feel "at home."

The Female Domain

In stereotypical representations of women's virtues enacted in a women's domain, the home is seen as the site for care, solicitude and love. In these narratives that connection holds true; however, the terrain of family relations, like the family itself, is expanded far beyond any narrow, privatized borders. In an emblematic description of her childhood home, one woman remembers that house as a site for the construction of meaning in middle of a world literally at war. But, in her telling, the house is the very opposite of an involuted, claustrophobic female retreat. It is the male parent who remains inside in this story. And, like the music her father plays, the meaning generated by the world-within flows into the world-without, breaching the boundaries constructed by the state.

> Probably the most influential thing I would guess in my life, in those days, when I was a kid growing up, was that both my parents were musicians. My mother was a, professional singer, and my father was her accompanist. And that just meant that music was going to be an important part of my life. For *me* as well as for others. So, that's been a kind of thread right straight through.
>
> You know, I was reflecting the other day with a friend that, in our house where we grew up, on ———— Street, the one with this great front porch, and during the Second World War when there would be air raid drills, we used to sit on the front porch, which was very illegal, 'cause you're all supposed to be in the basement. And, he would sit inside and play the piano. All during this time. And so it was like, we had the best of both worlds really. Sneaking around on the porch, watching all these air raid wardens in their white hats and he was playing the piano.

Even when the home has been established as the domain of women, this site need not necessarily stand on the margins of the social world. It can even be the nexus of the social activities for the larger religious community, as Elisabeth Schussler Fiorenza (1985) suggests in her *Feminist Theological Reconstruction of Christian Origins*. In an analysis which shows a high degree of correspondence with the discourse being discussed here, Fiorenza (pp. 286–288) examines the historical conditions under which the early Church shifted its organizational center from the "house church," characterized by communal authority and a central role for women, to the "household of God," with authority vested in the patriarchially defined office of bishops, and women's leadership relegated to marginal positions. In the early Church, as in present times, the feminist religious discourse suggests, the Church is faced with two competing models of family and home, and the more powerful patriarchal structure wins.

The irony of church organization is that the marginality of Catholic women religious has also given them a great degree of autonomy. It can be argued that, in spite of an overarching patriarchal structure, Catholic women religious have continued to maintain the alternative model of family and home within their gender-segregated space. This model underlies the narrative accounts of recent structural changes in the nuns' immediate surroundings. While still maintaining an environment in which women and women's values are at the center, they have broken their cloistered isolation from the larger society by moving into "ordinary houses" in local neighborhoods; and by living in community with their "clients," in shelters for the homeless and in therapeutic communities. One definition of the home is as a hub of ideologically compatible activity.

Teachers Working for Social Change

"I have been a teacher, *in some way or another,* for forty-five years." The emphasis which I have placed on these words (the opening of one woman's narrative,) summarizes all of these women's relationships to education. Teaching for these women is much more than employment in a school. When they find themselves unable to construct social meaning within the narrow confines of parochial schools, they abandon that environment. Working *outside* that established system, and, supported directly by persons of conscience, these women are able to address the particular material and moral needs of those around them.

Helping street people to get social security and find an apartment; giving women in prison a feminist interpretation of the Bible and electrical training; providing counselling for Catholic religious; conducting workshops on peace and social concerns; composing works of art with religious themes, all of these activities are redefined as teaching in its largest social sense. For those who are directly affected by these changes, as well as for those of us who read about them, these women are authors of new social relations and new social meanings. One of the most valuable contributions of this discourse is the way in which it expands our sense of progressive possibilities, in educational theory and practice.

4

A Pragmatic Discourse of Secular Jewish Women Teachers Working for Social Change

Introduction

Two specific groups of progressive activists inspired the original plan for this study. I was intrigued by fleeting references to dismissals of suspected communist teachers. Lader (1979: 79), for example, notes that, in the fifties,

> in New York City, 100 teachers were forced to resign although there was not proof that they had tried to indoctrinate their students. Many were reinstated in the 1970s after the laws sanctioning their dismissals were declared unconstitutional by the U.S. Supreme Court in 1967 and 1968.

I wondered who these teachers were and what had become of them.

And I was myself a member of the so-called "sixties generation," and was bemused by the various reports of its political demise. I wished to compare progressive women activists' own evaluations of their lives to popular media announcements that the "rebellious adolescents" of the sixties' generation were "all grown up" (Baruch, Barnett and Rivers, 1984: 100); "not crazy any more," "settled," "conservative," (Simrose, 1985: 1); and "reaping the rewards of working within the system" (Bladow, 1981: 57).

I also wanted to explore different assessments of political events among progressives. Many histories of the American left, it seems to me, are written from an implicit military perspective, focusing on male leaders (the "generals"), debating their confrontational strategies ("battle plans"), and equating the dissolution of organizations ("armies") with the failure of the political project (the "war"). In one such recent analysis, Miller's (1987) *Democracy is in the Streets*, the author refers to past participants as "veterans" of the movement, and quotes Tom Hayden: "We should be happy we came here, fought and survived. When they injure us, we will be warriors" (p. 304).

In contrast, Vivian Gornick (1977), who focuses on ordinary members of the Communist Party, and the relationship between their moments of political activism and the rest of their lives, uses existential language, and metaphors of "romance" and passion. Sara Evans' (1980) account of ordinary women participating in the Civil Rights, New Left and Women's Movements, is tinged with the irony of their search for a "free space" in their personal and political lives. So too, the discourse of the women in this study, as I will show, contains distinctive metaphors, understandings and evaluations.

Central, then, to my initial definition of progressive activism was a hypothetical woman teacher who had been a member of "Old" or "New" Left organizations or movements. As my research progressed it became increasingly clear that the "progressive women activists" to whom I was being referred did not fit the orthodox standards proposed. In the narratives of women in this study, for example, "communism" is, as a general rule, either omitted or explicitly rejected in connection with the "totalitarianism" and "imperialism" of the Soviet Union and China. Narrators report the use of the label "communist" as an insult and assault against progressive activists. One black woman, who was willing to call herself a communist, produced a unique coinage, combining it with her commitment to the Rastafarian movement in Jamaica.

There are several explanations for my difficulties in finding a coherent cohort of "classically" Left women teachers. Some of these reasons were related to my own biography. Unlike Gornick, I did not grow up in an activist milieu. My undergraduate years were spent at a conservative Catholic college, and I had become quite disconnected from my age-mates while living for long periods overseas. Hence, my immediate personal network in this country did not include many of the kind of women I wished to interview.

This was not simply a logistical problem. Several times I did make initial, albeit distant, contacts with former members of the Communist Party, but none of these lead to interviews. The need for trust between the researcher and the subject, accentuated by the project's explicitly political emphasis, was irredeemably jeopardized by the remoteness of my connections and the historical repression of the group I wished to study. Judging from my experiences with personal referrals, if I had traced the dismissed New York City teachers through relevant documents, a different project which I did not choose to pursue, it is questionable whether those women would have been willing to be interviewed by a stranger.

It is also questionable whether those women would still feel connected to what was essentially a fifty-year-old political label. None of the former communists in Gornick's (pp. 24–25) study are now political activists; she describes them as having "remade their lives." One former Communist Party member to whom I wrote responded: "I have spoken to a number of my friends about your project—all of whom have been reluctant to cooperate for one reason or another. Several others have died—and one suffers from memory deficit. So, regretfully, I can't be of help and I am truly sorry." As she had never been a teacher, this woman was not herself part of the study. But, her return envelope was sealed with "Save the Whales" stickers—an indication of the changes in her own political concerns since the thirties. So too, the present activities of women from the "sixties' generation," including those who had such apparent commonalities as participation in Students for a Democratic Society (SDS), now covered a wide and diverse political spectrum.

Although a Communist Party continues to exist, its membership, its structure, and the historical context have changed to such an extent that one could argue it is an entirely different organization than it once was. National, regional and local left-wing organizations, SDS, Schachtmanite Trotskyists, radical teachers' groups, all wax and wane in the narratives of this group. Indeed, I was most often referred to women on the basis of their former membership in disbanded organizations or networks which now exist only in fragmentary or reconstructed forms. If there is a continuity to the last fifty years of the American Left history, it is not institutional.

Evans traces an historical continuity in the persons of those progressive women who were successively engaged in the Civil Rights, New Left and new feminist movements, maintaining commitment, developing consciousness, and increasing organizational skills. One woman in this study, who was also interviewed by Evans, perceives such a pattern in her life. But Evans' developmental configuration cannot fully explain why women of apparently similar origins take divergent paths.

The political projects outlined by Evans, as well as her interview timetable, precede the narratives of this study by at least a decade, and her analysis is rooted in the seventies, at a particular moment in the Women's Movement. The picture of the American political Left in the eighties which emerged from my search for progressive women teachers, and from the narratives of whose I found, is one of indeterminate identities and latent connections. These women do not present themselves, and nor are they currently recognized, as a coherent entity in the larger public space.

In light of these collected narratives, I began to reconsider my own reconstruction of the past which, it seemed, equated political identity with organizational membership, and public confrontation with political action. The narratives, unlike my own original research design, present the complexities and ambiguities of long-term commitments to progressive political causes. They recount the continually shifting conditions within which the narrators must participate and to which they must respond; they include both instances of empowerment and periods of inaction.

Historical Questions; Pragmatic Answers

Given the contemporary absence of a grand political project, of strong institutional structures, of definitive political lines and of clearly orthodox identities among the American Left, I was nevertheless able to assemble a group of women who demonstrated a collective political understanding. In addition to their participation in projects of the Left, these five women share a secular Jewish background, and teaching experiences in inner-city public schools. Their discourse, while loosely articulated, consistently combines symbolic remembering of a common progressive history with an ongoing pragmatic perspective.[18]

History is a central concern of these narratives: each woman identifies herself as a one-time student of that academic subject, and as a past participant in major public events; each presents herself as a qualified chronicler of some part of the story of the American Left. But the making of history, whether in the construction of narrative accounts, or through involvement in activist projects, is not unproblematic.

As historians of their own lives, these women see the past through the lens of the present, and current contractions of possibility cast an ironic light on earlier visions of transformation. Every historian must grapple with the dynamics of change, but unlike theorists of the sixties and seventies who were puzzled by a seemingly sudden and conspicuous rise of militancy, these contemporary thinkers need to explain its apparent decline. As engaged historians, these women also need to reconcile their own participation in a continually changing series of political projects with their self-declared, consistently progressive, political agenda.

In their explicit self-appraisals, as well as in their constituative structuring of the life histories, these speakers answer the major historical questions which are raised by the narratives with pragmatic solutions: personal identity can only be established through participation in concrete political projects, but because some aspects of the social environment resist transformation, and others are in flux, activists must be ingenious and adaptive.

The Pragmatic Self and the Progressive Tradition

Throughout the narratives of this group, political self-definition is both a compelling and an impossible task. While all the participants in this study accepted the broad categorization of their political orientation as progressive, many, including members of this group, were hesitant to submit to any more specific "traditional" classification. The political self-namings that individuals in this group would (hesitantly) accept are so diverse and inconsistent (ranging from "Marxist" to "liberal-Left"), it is not surprising that several of them question the accuracy of any political label at the present time.

In their narratives, two women puzzle over the available alternatives, placing qualifications even on those who seem more appropriate. One explains:

> Well, I use the word progressive. Um, which is . . . Who knows what that means? When I say progressive, I do not mean liberal. Radical seems like an outdated term, and in fact, I feel like the right has taken it over in some ways, and so . . . it, you know, I . . . There aren't . . . there isn't a good term . . . I really feel as though the right has successfully co-opted so much of our language.

The other debates:

> I feel more comfortable with Marxist. I guess I am a socialist. I'm a socialist, yeah. Yeah. I feel comfortable saying that I'm a

socialist. Although, I would . . . I mean, that's between the two of us. I would *never* come out and say that . . . Actually . . . I don't . . . I don't ordinarily use the word Marxist either, actually . . . I would *never* wanna be labelled. I think my friends know where I stand. But I don't even say with friends . . . I don't even say like, "Well as a Marxist, you know, I believe in such and such. . . ."

Another woman remarks upon the irony of maintaining a label from the past, knowing that it will probably be misinterpreted in the present context: "I still call myself socialist. Which is good! It's likely, it's just as likely to mislead. I mean it is true; it's likely to . . . mislead people."

But *naming* is not as important as *doing;* at the same time that these narratives dismiss the vocabulary of partisan divisions, they describe their common progressive perspective in the language of pragmatism. In an epigrammatic expression of her own orientation to the social world, one woman sets forth the core concerns of this group's discourse: "I think it's partly a very strong tradition I had of, you know, you have to stay in the world the way it is, and you change the world. You need to work *in* the society."

In this woman's narrative, a pragmatic emphasis on immersion in, interaction with, and transformation of the social environment, is attributed to the tradition of socialist politics. "You are supposed to be where the working class is," she explains. In another specific example, she recalls her reactions to a teachers' strike: "I voted against the strike, but also, to keep with tradition, you went on strike. If that's what the majority of people wanted." By virtue of its connection to pragmatism, and in relationship to the other parts of this narrative, the word "tradition" here takes on a decidedly anti-absolute, antidogmatic, antiauthoritarian, antisectarian meaning.

The Pragmatic Self and the Jewish Tradition

In a virtual echo of the previous woman's definition of the socialist tradition, another women's account posits the Judaic tradition as the source of her pragmatic orientation:

There are at least two . . . streams of thought in Judaism. Or traditions. But definitely one of the traditions is a kind of tradition about that you, you know, this is the world we live in.

And the way that you prove you're a good man or a good
woman is by dealing with this world. There's no question that
that's part of what I believe.

Noting that her family "did *not* come out of formal religious training,"
she stresses the immanent focus of her morality: "I really believe that
you do your good deeds here, day-to-day, you know, and you don't
stock up points for afterlife. There's no question that's a part of the
Jewish tradition."

Other narratives make this same point of defining Jewish identity in
secular terms. One woman stresses the disjuncture between her earlier
religious training and her present cultural identity:

I don't remember so much the religious aspects, although I did
go to Saturday school and Sunday school until . . . I think until
I graduated from high school. But I don't remember anything
from that. I'm not proud of that fact either. But I don't remember that kind of thing. But I consider myself Jewish. More culturally.

Emphasizing the nonreligious nature of her Jewish upbringing, another
woman calls the creation of this identity critical to her political development.

My folks were not very religious Jewish, but they were very
identified. I mean they identified themselves very clearly as Jewish. It was not like the family did a lot of going to services or
that kind of stuff. There was a lot of talk about being Jewish
and what that meant. And for me politically that turned out to
be very important. I mean it was the beginning really of thinking about the world.

It also guided the initial direction of her intellectual development: "I
was good at all my subjects, and I didn't know how to pick, and I
knew they needed scientists in Israel, and so, I was gonna go and be a
math major and move to Israel. That was literally the plan I went to
college with."

But this is the only reference any of the women makes to Zionism,
and this woman is the only one to report an experience of anti-Semitism. Jewish identity is not an elaborated theme of these narratives; it
seems to be largely taken for granted. And, although an implicit overlap
of socialist and Jewish traditions emerges across the narratives, one

which has historical antecedents among European immigrants to this country, none of these narratives refers to that earlier phase of history, and none explicitly explains the connection between the two strands of thought.

Taken as a whole, the narratives do not reveal any necessary link between Judaism and progressive politics.[19] One woman relates that her parents were active in socialist and Jewish causes, but several other references suggest quite a different kind of combination. One woman mentions that her mother was a refugee from Europe to explain why that fearful parent forbade her to engage in political activity during her undergraduate years; another woman whose parents were antagonistic to student activism remembers her mother arranging for her to live in a private (and conservative) Jewish dorm when she went to college. The daughter of politically indifferent parents only refers to her Jewish background in connection with the "upper-middle-class, sixty percent Jewish" suburb in which she was raised.

Within the logic of these narratives, the pragmatic meanings which have been assigned to fragments of common cultural background are far more important than are the traditions themselves. These women do not rely upon precedents; they scrutinize available traditions, and select only those parts and combinations which correspond to their agenda. As one woman says:

> There are a lot of ways of thinking about the world. And I
> don't think in fact that any one of them is right. We can never
> know the whole thing. We can never understand it entirely,
> and which perspective we look at, which lens we look through
> depends on what our . . . agenda is in life.

The origins of a pragmatic perspective are not to be found in tradition, a pragmatist would argue; it must be referred back to the context within which it developed and in relationship to which it must be known and appraised.

In these narratives, the development of a pragmatic self takes place in the course of specific lived experiences, in distinctive places, and at particular times. It is important to specify what kinds of experiences these women do recall and how they remember them, because of the ways in which the popular media has construed the adventures of the larger group of which these activists are a part. By virtue of the kind of activities in which these women engaged, the times and places in which they did so, and the various interpretations which have since been made, one cannot escape discussing their lives in terms of so-called "sixties' activism."

The Pragmatic Self and Sixties' Activism

If sixties' activism is to be defined in terms of a particular age-group experiencing the same events at the same point of the life span, then, technically speaking, the women in this group do not comprise a generation, or a "cohort," as that term has been used by Elder (1977; 1981). The oldest of these women is now in her fifties; the youngest, in her thirties; only the three others who are in their forties qualify for such a categorization, their college years having coincided with the 1960s. This is, of course, the result of a deliberate decision on my part to test the explanatory power of a vertical versus a horizontal division of historical time.

The synchronism of demography, chronology, and political action necessary to the notion of a militant decade has limited importance in these women's own interpretations of their lives. Although there are, of course, several descriptions of that historical period in these stories, those women who could have been included in such a category do not *center* their life histories around that time, nor, do they, to give just one example, give much attention to the demonstrations for which that phase is now (in)famous. Furthermore, in spite of their generational differences, the narratives of those women who belong to different age-groups *are connected* to those of the "sixties" women in other, very significant, ways.

According to Davis (1979: 111), a generation is not assembled automatically; the memory of an age-group must be ideologically reconstructed through nostalgia, which "mediates the selection, distillation, refinement, and integration of those scenes, events, personalities, attitudes, and practices from the past that makes an identifiable *generation* of what would otherwise remain a featureless demographic cohort." It is clear that a great deal of "ideological reconstruction" has taken place with regard to the sixties' cohort, a reconstruction in which the interpretations of dominant groups have dominated.

The choice of a central conceptual category which mechanically slices political time into ten-year pieces, and the enormous emphasis placed on the numerical mass and age of the participants (with the accompanying idea of a "baby boom"), anticipates a kind of "natural" and necessary closure to this "stormy," "immature" phase. The persistent concentration on public confrontations, with particular stress on the actions of white, male, university students, distorts the race, gender, class and age configurations of the larger political constituencies involved. Such a explanation also obscures the actual continuities of political activism across the fifties, sixties and seventies, which Evans and others have documented, and, it distracts attention from all other interpretations of the causes of political action.

Of course, the life histories of the women in this group do contain elements which could also be found in a "sixties' generation" interpretation, but different principles of combination and interpretation are clearly at work. Campus activism, as it appears in these narratives, is not a singular, short, or spectacular political experience, but is presented as one of a series of practical political projects undertaken by these women within the educational institutions where they are located.

Before, during and after college, as students, as teachers, as neighbors, and as parents, these women act upon the pressing problems of their immediate social context; and, since they have spent so much of their lives in educational environments, their narratives present a kind of catalogue of recent progressive struggles over schooling in America.

The Pragmatic Self and Student Activism

Segregated schools were, of course, an early, and major, target of the Civil Rights Movement. In her life history narrative, one woman tells how she participated in this political project as a sixteen-year-old high school student in the schools of Washington, D.C. She explains the background of the problem in this way: "Washington did not have home rule and didn't have a mayor at that point. It had *nothing*. We were totally controlled by this one committee in Congress that was run by racists. Southern Democrats. And as a consequence, the schools were a real disaster. It was shameful, really." And, she describes the personal effects of her own involvement:

> I went to the whitest schools, and the best schools in the system, because of the neighborhood, from the time I was in junior high on. But I *did* know enough about the city from my earlier years, and I got involved with this group of high school students from every school in the city. So it was an integrated group. And we lobbied Congress, you know, as sixteen year olds. We went in interracial teams. And that was a tremendous

eye-opener to me, because we were not allowed in the offices of
a lot of Congressmen.

I learned a lot. The combination of all these political things
happening to me was very meaningful. Going to all these con-
gressional meetings, and trying to get into Congressmen's offices, and the racism we were confronted with, and the funda-
mentalism, and this one guy lectured us for an hour on the
Bible. I can remember that stuff now, I mean, we are talking
twenty, twenty years ago, very vividly. It was a *very* important
experience. I went off to college with all of that sort of, kind of
germinating in my head, and my politics really ready to burst.

In a pragmatic reading of this initial political "experiment," one
could point out how, in her active interaction with her social environment, this woman encountered a problematic situation that interfered
with her development; how she became a member of a group collec-
tively engaged in a problem-solving activity; and how she was able to
add elements of the solution to her reserves of experience.

What is interesting about this woman's construction, and similar
formulations in the other narratives, is the way in which the process
of political growth is described in highly energized, almost violent,
terms. The larger social environment presented in these narratives is
consistently conflictual, with the narrators repeatedly challenged by a
seemingly endless succession of crises. Yet, intermingled with the sense
of struggle against negative forces, positive feelings of excitement and
pleasure are also regularly expressed. For example, one woman recalls
her adolescent activism in this way: "I guess it was in junior high. I
went down to Washington, you know. And all those marches in the
city and things like that. It was, you know, half social, half . . . you
know, what a teenager did, and it was sort of fun." Another speaks
enthusiastically about her college activism:

> I remember we were getting our first apartment, and I was so
> excited about that. It was with a group of people that I really
> liked and they were very, all of them were very politically ac-
> tive. We were working on campus elections. They had a plat-
> form that included U.S. out of Vietnam. And there was some-
> thing about closing down fraternities at the time, I think.
> Anyways, we were working on that, and that was exciting.

All of the women in this group acknowledge the fact that the private
and public universities which they chose to attend (Swarthmore, Anti-

och, Bennington, Brandeis, the University of Chicago, Columbia University, and the University of Wisconsin) have the highest academic ratings; at the same time they point out the political qualities which attracted them to these institutions.

In her academically oriented family, one woman recalls, giving a typical description, "there was a whole hoopla around where I was gonna go to school. I knew I wanted to go to a really good college, and I felt like maybe I would meet, you know, more interesting people and stuff." What finally made up her mind to what seemed like an unusual choice, a small Quaker institution, was "the only thing I heard about it was that it was a place where you could go that, where, if you had been arrested, it wouldn't count against you. Well, *that* sounded like a really good place to go to college!"

In a similar vein, the youngest woman in the group decided to go to a university which was famous for its activism, although anti-war protests were winding down by the time she enrolled, because, "you know, it had a history that was *very* interesting to me, and very, sort of, romantically interesting." She became very active in local student and community politics.

In college, the oldest of these women jokes, "I think I was the last person to join a . . . any 'subversive,' 'radical' organization. In 1950, '50, I became a Trotskyist." Her narrative shows a chronological transition away from the agenda of the Old Left. By the time that she had finished university, she became politically involved, on a neighborhood basis, in problems of race and education.

As the phrases "Mississippi summer" and "Vietnam summer" (used by two women in this group) indicate, two major political crises punctuated student activists' college careers in the sixties. What has often been overlooked in analyses of these two overlapping issues is that educational problems were common to both.

For the woman who petitioned the Congress as a high school student, "it was a *very* easy transition" to SDS organizing in college. As a member of that campus-based group, she participated in a desegregation campaign in a nearby town. In a pattern which repeats itself not only in her life, but throughout this group of narratives, here again the issue was race; the terrain, schools; the strategy, pragmatic.

> The school system was still segregated. And it was lots of stuff that was very familiar to me from my school activism in Washington. So it was a very easy transition for me to kind of go into full SDS organizing. Leafleting housing projects, trying to pull together a group for better and more integrated schools.

And that was what we got involved in, and because it was such a racist city, there were immediately beatings and mass arrests. Which scared me a lot, because my folks had made it clear to me that I was not going to be allowed to stay in college if I got involved in anything. So I had to pull back . . . some. We helped organize a boycott of schools. And I would run freedom classes, you know. And I would try to stay out of direct confrontations with the police.

But, by 1965, this woman recalls, the Civil Rights Movement "wasn't quite the same"; "Black Power had happened." And, by that time, she had "already learned a lot about Vietnam, because there were people on campus who were active, and brought news of that kind of stuff pretty early on." One of her friends "went on to be the president of SDS, and then he travelled through Hanoi." In her words, "my mind was just bursting with all this stuff, and I was getting real active and interested."

As the war in Vietnam escalated, and the anti-war movement developed on campuses, students' analysis of the relationship between problems in the larger society and those within the university itself became increasingly more elaborated. Moving beyond the obvious self-interest of male students' vulnerability to the draft, students began to question connections between military funding and university research, the relationship between university real estate holdings and local community needs, the relations of production of university knowledge, even the nature of the university itself.

One consequence was a disintegration of authority relationships within the university; one woman recalls putting these ideas into practice.

(The professor) led a very loose class. And basically let us grade ourselves. This was 1970. There was this one guy in the class who really influenced me more than anyone else. I wouldn't consider him an anarchist, but he was very opposed to any kind of strict authority and discipline. And we decided to break way from the class, because we didn't like what they were talking about.

I remember taking over the class with him and a few other students. We brought in a video, and we locked the doors, and we told everyone that *we* were gonna teach the class that day, sort of mimicking what happens in most other classes, and we weren't gonna let any of the students have any input, and we were trying to provoke a fight. We ended up having a fight,

which we were very happy about. Just to prove our point.
That, in fact, the minority counts as well. In retrospect, it was
a little bizarre! But we were having fun.

Authority relations in education continue to be a pressing issue
throughout these narratives.

It is interesting to note that the women in this group do not ordinarily
attack the university itself in their stories, but rather tell a tale of a
satisfying educational experience during their college years, *albeit one
which was often extracurricular and extramural.* One woman goes so
far as to say, "I always felt that classes kind of got in the way. There
was so much, there were so many other things going on." But another
woman remembers particular professors she "loved listening to. I definitely felt like I was learning. And I felt like I was being challenged."
In any case, all the members of this group were academically successful,
and did receive their degrees.

Indeed, intellectual analysis and critical reflection are valued components of these women's political activism. One woman remembers
being immediately attracted to the SDS because, as she thought at the
time, "these people know what they are talking about, and they have
an analysis." Another woman says, "I remember being in study groups,
and really learning about imperialism for the first time. I had never
understood what that meant." The criterion for judging worthwhile
learning seems to have been that it be socially built from shared information and experiences, and that it be relevant to an understanding of
the ongoing crises.

In more conventional academic terms, all of the women in this group
make a point of mentioning their academic studies of history, political
science, and sociology, and the impact of such books as Bowles and
Gintis' (1976) analysis of American education. And they continue to
have strong connections to the academic world; three of the older
women have taught university courses; and four out of the five women
in this group have pursued graduate degrees. In terms of friendship and
professional relationships, this group of teachers is closely connected to
the "academic base" of the American neo-Marxist tradition, and, as I
shall elaborate below, these women use a particular version of that
discourse in their narratives.

The Pragmatic Self and Community Activism

At several points in his history of the American Left, Lader criticizes
the "strategy" of the New Left in trying to shift its activities into the

"slums" (p. 176) or into "clerical offices and technical laboratories" (p. 230); in "abandoning its campus base" for "armed struggle" (p. 265). What Lader's construction of a faceless organization fails to take into account is that, as time went on, successive sets of students were finishing their degrees (or abandoning their studies altogether,) and so, as a necessary consequence, leaving the university environment. In these life histories, the departure from the university is a significant, even traumatic, transition; but, wherever these narrators live and work, a continuity of political activism and educational concerns persists in their narratives.

Describing her life after university, the oldest woman in this group observes, "I had a daughter in 1956, and that wasn't a very high point in American Left politics." But in the particular neighborhood where she lived, "if there was anything going on, we'd have something there." When the city initiated an urban renewal plan, "removing a lot of black people from the neighborhood," she got involved in public housing and civil rights issues.

Initially, she worked in the NAACP and CORE, anticipating by only a few years the interracial community activism of other women in this group. But "it became increasingly difficult" to work in such organizations, with "the whole issue of Black Power and the relationship of whites to the Civil Rights Movement." Subsequently, in connection with her own children's schooling (and independently of her teaching job in another district), she worked with a group of parents who succeeded in having tracking abolished in local integrated schools.

After graduation, one woman followed her husband to a midwestern city where he had a summer job. It was a politically distressing experience for her. "We were surrounded by very, very conservative people. And I knew some people who were in Mississippi summer and so it really sort of freaked me out, to be out there and to feel powerless." When they returned to a large city in the Northeast in the fall, she worked on the election campaign of a black mayoral candidate, and "eventually became involved in what became an SDS project. Doing welfare organizing, working with people about schools, very much local neighborhood issues, and learning a lot in the process. Trying to do it around interracial organizing."

Although she was no longer a student, almost all of the other organizers were. She uses an educationally and pragmatically oriented vocabulary to describe the experience and assess its effect:

But I was learning a lot. I was learning a lot about . . . what it meant to be poor, and what it meant to be a woman. Just learning how to be competent, and how to apply for certain things, and about bureaucracies. It was really an education for me. It was certainly a learning experience for me.

We were somewhat effective. We were able to help welfare mothers learn more about their rights, and to get food stamps. We were much more effective with women than with men. We were based around neighborhood things.

Soon after graduating, and after a short but disastrous public school teaching experience, one woman sought work in community organizing. She found both activities combined in a particular political project.

At the same time, I had moved to this neighborhood. And sort of was looking for a way to get involved in neighborhood organizing. And started asking around, and discovered, lo and behold, there was a group of people who not only were doing organizing in the area, but were starting a school. Which was the last thing I wanted to hear actually, at that point, but I was interested, and they were going to start a working class school.

Although one woman participated in a food co-op and a tenants' union after she graduated from college, as "a way to maintain a social network and remain politically active," like the other women in this group, she soon moved into more educationally oriented projects. She tutored low-income junior high students, and coordinated an after-school program for Hispanic children at a YMCA. She subsequently began her school teaching career doing career counselling with Hispanic high school students.

The Pragmatic Self and the Teaching Profession

Listening to these women's initial remarks on the teaching profession, it is wholly amazing to find that any of them ever become teachers. According to their narratives, whenever they were encouraged to be teachers, (as was usually the case, by their parents,) it was because they were young *women,* and teaching was seen as women's work, compatible with being a wife and mother. But precisely because of this gender stereotyping, and because of their own sense of intellectual worth, they all vigorously resisted.

It is remarkable to hear the same vehement phrases echoing in the narratives of individuals who have never met each other. One woman recalls her response to any suggestion that she become a teacher. "Over my dead body! Not me!"; another quotes herself saying, "Anything but a teacher!' I mean it was *so clear* to me that I was *never* going to be a teacher." "I said '*Never!*' The *last* thing I would do is teach children," one woman remembers. Another recounts: "The last thing in the world I ever wanted to be was a teacher, because I had such a stereotype in my mind. And women, I guess I thought they were teaching because they weren't allowed to do anything else." These sentiments are repeated by yet another woman: "I didn't have the slightest desire to be a teacher. Teaching was totally out of my mind. The only people I knew who took education courses were people who were dumb, or really looking for a quick fix."

When the oldest of these women *did* become a teacher in the fifties, it *was* the convenience of compatibility with child-rearing which was one of the occupation's main attractions. But when this same woman began to take education courses at a nearby university, she was forcefully discouraged by a faculty member: "He called me in to urge me to get out of elementary school teaching. And he was very indignant. He said 'Why do we educate women like you? Who end up teaching children. With your academic background, you should be doing something more important.' " Thirty years later, the youngest member of this group recalls a similar experience:

They said they were shocked at us. One was from Colgate, one from Wisconsin, and another from the New School. She had her doctorate. She was going back for education 'cause she wanted to. And we were all very high SAT people and they couldn't understand it, but they were delighted that we were there. They treated us very nicely.

But they didn't want us to be in the city system. They thought the city system was ridiculous. They wanted us to go into private schools or out of the city. Because they said, "You're going to have to put up with so much. You're not going to be able to teach, You'll be wasted there."

Why then did all these women chose to become teachers? Several kinds of practical explanations are presented in the narratives. To begin with, the transition from university entails much more than moving from a campus to a neighborhood; as explicitly stated by two women, the need to find paid employment is an urgent and upsetting problem which students anticipate even before they graduate. Puzzling over her inexplicable change from a sociology to an education major, one woman says, "I don't remember now why I switched. Probably because I figured I couldn't get a job." "Just out of the blue," in her senior year, says another woman, she began telling people that she was going to be a teacher. She reconstructs her explanation: "I'll be a teacher. I'll be able to earn money. Because my folks were quite clear that they were not supporting another month of my life. So, I knew I had to earn money, and teaching was a real option. So there I was! Off to be a teacher!"

But, of course, economic necessity can be satisfied in other kinds of work. The special attractions of teaching were, in several cases, historically specific. Although it was not one of her personal imperatives, one woman remembers that, "in the anti-war days," young men went into teaching because they "could get out of the draft." The indirect effect of this option on female graduates was that friends who graduated before them were already teaching in schools.

> I had a friend who had graduated the year before, who had moved up here, along with my boyfriend, and had become a teacher. And he kept coming back, and saying, "There's a lot of radical teachers. You could really come. You could get a sub job, and before you know it, you've got a teaching job." And we were gonna do lots of neat stuff in schools. I thought, this is great. There's a community of people; I can be with my boyfriend; there's a lot of Vietnam work going on in the area.

For the three women who chronologically belonged to the sixties' generation, teaching provided a continuity of their social networks, and an extension of their ongoing political projects. As one woman's narrative recalls, there was even a section of SDS called TDS, Teachers for a Democratic Society. She was doing SDS "power structure research for a neighborhood group" during her summer vacation in 1966, when she and a friend enrolled in their first education courses. Becoming a teacher seemed the natural thing for a student activist to do, and an acute teacher shortage meant that "those were the days you could literally walk into a school system and become a teacher."

The circumstances of the oldest and youngest women in the group differed from those of the sixties women; yet, common underlying themes emerge. The births of her three children created a kind of crisis for the first woman.

> I had three children. '56, '58, '60. And I began to have sudden trepidation about how many children I was gonna have! I was

very delighted having children. Having a child was the most marvelous experience. However, by 1960, I decided it was not the solution to all my problems. It sort of revived questions of what was I gonna do with my life.

By taking a part-time teaching job in a neighborhood school, she planned to make enough money "to hire some household help to do the things I didn't like to do around the house. Thereby leaving me freer to be with my children, and to do the kind of work I wanted to do," that is, unpaid political activism. Thus, she also gives practical personal, economic and political reasons for her choice.

The death of her mother created a crisis for the second woman. She had continued to work at a student job as a restaurant chef after graduation, and she describes how her life was drifting:

I loved cooking, but I started to feel stupid after awhile. It was work, and it was nice, sort of sweaty work, but I started to feel dumb. And also I started to drink a lot there, because, that's what you do. Because you have free drinks, and it's a social atmosphere, and after work you can sit with everybody, waiters, and actors and actresses, and the cooks. So, you know, I'd get home at three or four o'clock in the morning, and then just feel sort of . . . wasting my life away.

When she heard that her mother had cancer, she flew home the next day. Over the next two years, she did temporary work; then, as her mother got increasingly ill, she took over more and more of her care. After her mother died, she recalls, she tried to stay drunk for two weeks. Then, she quotes herself, "I said, 'I'm going to go get my master's and teach.'"

As she notes in her narrative, she was now unemployed, and had never really taken the necessary steps to find a professional job. She rejected the idea of becoming a lawyer because of her past disillusioning encounters with "egomanic" political personalities, but the decision precipitated by her mother's death was, nevertheless, clearly grounded in her previous intellectual and political experiences, for she chose to become a social studies teacher. Thus, like the other women in this group, she solved problems of personal meaning and political significance, and managed to earn her living at the same time, by choosing to become a teacher. In what is probably the most dramatic formulation of any in these narratives, she defines and defends this decision.

I Answer With My Life

> Why I'm in education and why I wanna be is . . . to change the
> world. And to change it with these kids, which is somewhat de-
> pressing, and it's frustrating. I think my view of the world is
> that some people have been put down and left out, politically,
> economically, psychologically, and I think that I could be some-
> one who could go there and start a few kids and make them
> not be that way anymore. And that's my idea of politics. And
> that's my view of the world, and I want to basically make peo-
> ple feel that they're stronger and freer and I think teaching is
> the way to do that. I sorta figure if I can make some of them
> feel like they have some kind of power in the world, I'll be
> happy.

Political Action and Working for Wages

Although, throughout these narratives, teaching is consistently constructed as a kind of work with the *potential* to satisfy these women's
financial requirements as well as their political intentions, it is neither
a ready-made nor a permanent solution to the tension between these
two needs. As previously noted, these women report that when they
engage in political action, they experience excitement, even pleasure.
However, the anticipation and the eventualities of *working for wages*
often provokes an opposite reaction. Consider, for example, the tensions in the following quotations from one woman's narrative: "I went
through a fairly unhappy period. Not quite wanting to be there. And
being active in the summer with Vietnam work, and a little bit during
the year. I'd go on marches. But having a (teaching) job made it hard";
"So that was going on, and the follow-up of the summer program was
going on, so I was real high off of all of this, but I was getting
increasingly broke, and needed to get a teaching job."

Throughout this particular woman's narrative, working for wages
as a public school teacher is an alienating experience. She tells, for
example, of teaching ancient history in a high school where students
drew swastikas on her books. When, however, she went to work at a
politically inspired alternative school, initially "for free, because they
couldn't pay me anything," and later, for very low pay, she had quite
a different experience.

The alternative school lasted for ten years, until it became impossible
to sustain financially. She describes this period (when, for her, working

for wages was temporarily transformed into creative political practice) with nostalgia, and mourns its loss:

> The school was this wonderful respite! Not having to worry about what I was doing. And just getting to do this work I really liked. But that will never happen again. Every few years you really have to face up again to, how am I gonna put this together, with my politics, interests and skills. You know. I don't think I'll ever find a job like that again.

At the time of her interview with me, she was working as a freelance consultant and writer on issues of public policy.

Some women in this group have been able to sustain the combination of work and politics for longer periods of time. Yet it is clear from all their narratives that, in the "normal" activities of the society in which they live, the "realm of necessity" has precedence over the "realm of freedom." In recent years, for example, several women note regretfully, the demands of jobs and family have left them with little "spare" time and energy to participate in demonstrations or other political activities, as they used to do. As one woman says,

> I've been quite overwhelmed by the amount of work I've had to do in the last number of years, 'cause I've really supported our family primarily. And having two kids. That's very hard for me to have to have political commitments on top of that. Even just doing the affinity group. Like this week there were two major demonstrations, and it was a wipeout. I had chicken pox at home, and you know, to try to even get down to those was . . . I did make it, but . . . Our affinity groups are a joke. You know, I can get arrested between nine and two on a Tuesday, but not on a Thursday.

The only practical solution which these women have found is, whenever possible, to combine the two realms in an educational-political project. For, however favorable or unfavorable the circumstances may be at any moment in time, the goals to which these women aspire can only be advanced through *practical human energy*, which is, of course, not infinite.

As this explication of the group's construction of the choice to be a teacher demonstrates, these women do not only use some of the vocabulary of the Left (for instance, "working class," "imperialism"); the way in which they perceive, organize and interpret their experiences corresponds to certain fundamental characteristics of Marxist theory and methodology. The basic concepts of "praxis" (here presented as political action) and "labor" (here presented as working for wages) are implicitly defined and elaborated upon through the use of concrete illustrations; and a relationship between them is explored. A correlative relationship between the "realm of freedom" and the "realm of necessity" is also implicitly examined.[20]

A central historical question has been constructed in the narration of each of these life histories: "How can I, living as I do, in history, subject to its changing conditions, and, given my own personal human needs, engage in free, creative and self-creative activity, to create, make, produce, change, and shape my historical, human world, and myself?"[21] How, in other words, can I engage in political activity, when, on the one hand (to give one example) white participants are no longer welcomed in the Civil Rights Movement, and on the other hand (to give another) I need to financially support myself and my family? A paraphrase of Marx's famous quotation provides an answer: "I can make history, but I cannot make it just as I please; I cannot make it under circumstances of my own choosing, but only under circumstances directly encountered, given and transmitted by the past."

The Language of Labor[22]

The Marxist concept of *labor,* here used in its most inclusive sense, also provides an answer. Unique to these pragmatic narratives (which present neither a "realistic" description of "what is," nor an "idealistic" projection of "what ought to be") is a sense of *what is possible,* through the *necessary and useful application of human energy,* through *labor.*

However difficult and alienating the conditions under which they must labor, these women consistently see their educational work as a socially and politically useful and necessary application of human energy. Indeed, the particular implicit construction of teaching which is presented in these narratives closely coincides with Sewell's (1980: 277) description of the "socialist vision of labor as the constituent activity of the social and political order." Labor stands as the central organizing concept in these women's narratives, and the (implicit) metaphor of teacher as artisan stands at the center of their system of symbolic representations.

The Teacher as Artisan

Teacher as worker is, of course, an implicit metaphor in the discourse of dominant theorists, representing an embodiment of the standardization, quality control, and technical efficiency which they value. And it is the same metaphor explicitly critiqued by critical theorists, who associate it with mechanization, exploitation and lack of human meaning.[23]

The teachers in this group do share some important common roots with the left-wing academic tradition; I have already suggested some of the reasons why in the first part of this chapter. Nevertheless, it is necessary to explore the ways in which these women's language does (and does not) correspond to university-generated versions, to examine the conditions under which it has developed over time, and to show the particular enrichments these women's articulations can bring to the discourse as a whole.

In the version of teacher as worker constructed by these women, there is a critique of existing practice, but there is also an unexpected presentation of the positive possibilities of such an identity. In contrast to the two versions above, the intriguing reconstruction which these narratives present is not that of a *factory* worker, but one which I have called "teacher as artisan."[24]

What has emerged from the "enormous proliferation of research on the history of working people" in the past twenty years, according to Sewell (p. 1), is "almost universal agreement on one point: that skilled artisans, not workers in the new factory industries, dominated labor movements during the first decades of industrialization." If, as Sewell (p. 1) and others argue, "the nineteenth-century labor movement was born in the craft workshop, not in the dark satanic mill," then the choice of the artisan metaphor has a kind of symbolic authenticity in a discourse which emphasizes political activism.

What such a metaphor does not resolve, however, is what Sewell (p. ix) calls the "intriguing but little-noticed paradox" of the discourse of revolutionary workers "laced with seemingly archaic terminology." As I present the details of this construction, I will continually attempt to explain why women in a postindustrial society use referents from a "mode of production" twice removed. In their interpretation, it seems, there are kinds of doing and making which never become obsolete.

What also needs to be explained about the use of such referents is their apparent removal from any gender context. As Melosh (1982: 8) has noted, the history of artisans and skilled workers, such as weavers, shoemakers or machinists, is, almost by definition, the history of men's work. This version of feminism, it seems, adopts a male prototype as the basis of its symbolic system. These women have always collaborated with men on educational-political projects, and it is one of their assumptions that they are as capable as any male co-worker. They talk about instances of discrimination, for example, there being only five female high school principals in a large northeastern state, as if they were illogical and somewhat bizarre.

Professional Expectations; Proletarian Experiences

It is clear that these women do not labor under circumstances of their own choosing. Their narratives record sharp contradictions: the set of expectations engendered by their families' professional backgrounds, and their own elite educations are in direct conflict with the continual pressure they feel to earn a living, and the actual working conditions which they experience. In a particularly bitter remembrance of her initiation to teaching, one woman protests:

> I have never in my life liked this school system, where I have
> been treated so much like a child. And there certainly was from
> the very start an *enormous* rage in my heart, strictly personal
> rage at how I was treated. From the first time that I went to
> get certified and was shouted at by matrons and, you know,
> you had to carry your urine sample, and I mean the whole
> thing, the impersonal, debasing way in which you were treated.
> It enraged me.

The shock of these contradictions becomes one source of these women's hybrid artisan identity. They regularly testify to the intensity and efficacy of their labor (they are conscientious workers) but they also continually demand the autonomy of higher-status jobs, and make a point of publicizing the degree of their intellectual expertise (for they are also unacknowledged professionals).

In their descriptions of their family backgrounds, these women admire the autonomy which they believe that their parents (and, in some cases, siblings, and spouses) have experienced in their occupations, emphasizing the fact that these relatives are either independently employed or freelance professionals. One woman explicitly compares herself to her "semiprofessional" podiatrist father: "He ran his own office. A one-man office, no nurse, no anything. I've thought about it

a lot. What kind of role model I had in him. Because he was autono-
mous. He *never* had a boss. And that turned out to be important in
my career." After ten years of teaching in an alternative school, she
continues, ten years "of being my own boss, teaching whatever I
wanted, making up my own curriculum, running my classes anyway I
wanted, I *just* couldn't face going into the public schools."

In other examples, one woman's father "was a salesman, and had a
company of his own, actually"; and another woman envies her husband (who "is not a suit and tie person") because he can work at home.
What these descriptions also acknowledge, however, is that these people are somehow involved in the world of business, a world which
these women explicitly reject.

Working one summer for a publishing company, one woman recalls,
she was "in a screaming rage" because she had never before "felt
discriminated against as a woman," and she knew she "*couldn't exist
in a corporate world.*" "It is quite clear to me I would never be happy
working in business. Because I feel like I have to be doing something
of social value," announces another woman, whose husband "says
that one person in the family is enough to dealing with that kind of
lack of meaning." Thus, while these women have politically distanced
themselves from the (broadly defined) class of their origins, they are
still, in varying degrees, dependent upon that socio-economic group in
important ideological and financial ways.

There are also sharp contradictions between the schooling which
these women have experienced, and that which is available to the
students they teach. The shock of this comparison was a moment of
political enlightenment for one woman: "I always knew something
was amiss where I was growing up. But I didn't know how to focus
my energy or how to rebel, exactly. I remember taking this one course
in urban education, and I had no idea about what it was like, and it
was really an eye-opener to me." She remembers her early experiences
as a substitute teacher with wonderment.

And, in retrospect, it really amazes me, that I would go into
some of these areas blindly the way I did. I would just go. I
was so naive I didn't know what I was doing. I was just trying
to get to school on time. And not being that successful at that
either! Now, after teaching for so many years, I would never
go into the projects alone now. *Never!*

For another woman, being a substitute teacher in the inner city
confirmed her worst judgments about the schooling of children of
color, and those living in poverty. For herself,

well, it was a *fabulous* education. I went to everything from kindergarten through high school. And I went to *every* school in the city, just about. And, you know, I saw schools, I just couldn't believe how bad they were. It reinforced experiences that I had growing up, and what I had seen in my college town. Over and over again just seeing these *horrible* conditions that black kids and poor kids were being educated in. It was just *disgusting*.

She jokes about making pragmatic decisions when she was told to teach cooking to a vocational education class without access to a kitchen:

This is a joke to anyone who knows me because I *do not* cook. And the last sub they'd had had been locked in the closet. So there was this classical situation: these very poor girls, very tough, no kitchen, and they'd signed up to learn cooking as a trade. *My* solution was to let them do whatever they wanted, because I didn't wanna be locked in the closet. So, of course, we got along really well. And the girls would ask personal questions, sex, you know. And I discovered that they were hungry. So we would sneak down into the cafeteria, and under the pretext of, 'we're the cooking class,' we would make sandwiches for ourselves and eat.

Her observations are confirmed by a woman who worked in another large city.

I got a sense of what *wasn't* happening in schools. A large number of the classes that I subbed in were classes that had nothing but subs. There were a few classes in *every* school that had *no* regular, full-time teacher. And they had no materials, and no supplies and no program whatsoever.

The Journey-Person

In their detailed accounts of substitute teaching, these women give a great deal of significance to this experience, creating, in the telling, a metaphor of a "journey-person," who travels from place to place, earns a daily wage, and perfects the skills of the trade through wide-ranging, hands-on practice. As already committed progressive activists, an essential task for these women is the development of a politically appropriate teaching repertoire.

One woman remembers how, as a substitute teacher, she "could rummage around teachers' desks," "go to the teachers' lunchroom and listen to conversations," "open doors, or peer in their windows." But it was easier to see what was wrong than to know what to do yourself; she was uncomfortable with what she observed of veteran teachers' practice, and appalled by her own amateur attempts.

> At one point, I hit a kid. The thing that shocked me was I had always been good with kids. I mean, I hadn't been interested in teaching, or working with children, but I had always been naturally good with kids. And I had worked with adolescents, and I liked adolescents, and I assumed that I was naturally gonna have no trouble.
>
> So the amount of rage and anger I felt at even five-year-olds staggered me. And the amount of frustration that I felt directly towards kids. And the amount of tension, in the schools, the general tone of fear and tension, the trepidation that everything was gonna fall apart at any moment. A concentration of control that I felt internally myself, and the only thing was could I survive this day, could I control this group of kids. And the amount of struggle that was required in that control.

"Progressive" Education

By her own account, this woman was determined to understand and act upon her teaching problems: "I think I was more dangerous in the classroom than if they had been left by themselves!" and "I couldn't just say, 'well, it doesn't matter.' " As she recalls, several factors contributed to her own education as a teacher. First of all, she was given a regular kindergarten teaching job. Then, she found out that, "to my surprise, teaching kindergarten kids was . . . it was very exciting, very interesting. And learning how schools might be organized, and how children's language develops, and the relationship of language and social status. I mean, *everything,* from *every* point of view." And, she began reading books, "Like Sylvia Ashton-Warner's" (1963), to help her develop her perspective. Living in three different cities, she continued to teach, read, and, and eventually, write about education.

I Answer With My Life

For a long time, teaching "was an entirely private enterprise," one that she "was fascinated with," but one that she could not explain to disinterested friends and colleagues. Finally, she became part of a university-sponsored teachers' workshop project based on open education, and was able to "resolve" her "mixed feelings." With the help of a mentor, "the first person (she) knew who could put it all together," she saw how to combine "respect for the craft of teaching, and child development, and thinking about learning, and political understanding."

In the sixties and seventies, open education was adopted by many educators who were looking for a politically progressive model of education, for the solutions it offered to problems of knowledge and authority in schools seemed to be distinctive alternatives to those which were promulgated by the dominant ideology. Given this trend, together with the fact that the "open" model and its "experimentalist" philosophy share an historical overlap with "pragmatic" thought (as in the work of Dewey), it is not surprising to find that all of the women in the group discovered this way of doing things. Different aspects of this perspective appear throughout the narratives, in concrete examples, as well as in explicit formulations of values. The following statement by this same woman is but one such instance:

> Where neither the teacher nor the student have much influence
> about what goes on in the classroom . . . That is, it seems to
> me, real dominant today. And I think it has been since the six-
> ties. A lot of teacher and student input . . . That's the kind of
> education I'm looking for. You can call it open, progressive,
> whatever you wanna call it.

Making Curriculum

The cooperative labor of teacher-artisans and the assistance of their apprentice-students are absolutely necessary in this kind of education, for, from these teachers' point of view, curriculum must be constantly renewed if knowledge is to be relevant and useful.

Such assumptions are evident in these teachers' disdain for all decreed or prepackaged materials. The youngest woman in this group is interested in creating her own lessons, and planning the whole year around "one great concept like revolution" (an interesting choice!); such a project "would be delightful." Instead, she says, "they give me"

96

a ready-made curriculum; she drops it entirely whenever she gets a chance. "We were discussing today what a typical teenager is. And I asked them to write an essay. From these repeater kids, I just got amazing stuff."

The same assumptions also hold true with reference to these women's own work, which they see as being immediately relevant, but quickly outmoded. One woman talks about a Vietnam curriculum she worked on:

> I actually have a copy of this that I brought up for you from the basement. I just rescued it from a barn where the last ex- isting fifty copies were being stored. And they were about to be thrown all out. You see everything is really rusted. This is *so* out of date. We did this in 1967. I'm not going to force this on you. I can't imagine you'd have any use for it.

Yet these women spend a large proportion of their narratives describing the *tangible products* of their labor. An examination of these accounts reveals important aspects of their thinking about work.

In the course of our interviews, women in this group would often proudly present me with copies of their work. Of course, the existence of material objects demonstrates workers' efforts in a measurable form, and this general sense of the need for a public justification of one's work is not absent from these stories. "I've done nothing but write for the last three or four years, and I've got a stack of products," says one woman who misses the social dynamics of teaching. According to another woman, writing is a more legitimate activity than teaching, in the eyes of her professional and intellectual associates: "I partly wrote because I wanted to make what I was doing respectable. 'Cause in my view of life, it was respectable if you could write about it!" Written works are also seen as contributions to the creation of a progressive discourse: "Being able to put out this book that's gone nationally and is in the hands of advocates all over the country and stuff about the economy and so. I feel real good about that. That was a way of using my politics very effectively."

What distinguishes these products in the eyes of their makers is the sense in which they do not belong to the system of commodified exchange. One woman explicitly describes the distribution of a radical teachers' newspaper in these terms:

> We would write these articles, and we would put it together, and put it out as a newspaper, and then we would distribute it

in much the same way as we had distributed the Vietnam curriculum. We would go to schools. And just talk to teachers and hand it out, and use our networks of teachers to make sure it got in the teachers' room of every school. And we had a circulation of over six thousand. Which was pretty good! Most of them we gave out free.

Unfortunately, this system can create practical problems. "It stopped coming out. We just couldn't sustain it anymore. Which was really too bad, because it did have this great circulation and we just . . . stopped." Both energy and money are in limited supply. For some of these women's products, such as journal articles, their own "surplus labor" is sufficient; for others, like curriculum projects, donations and grants have to be found. But, because this is political work, the alienating effects of the cash nexus do not seem to operate, whatever the actual sources of funds.

For these women, both intellectual skills and physical labor are involved in the curriculum creation process, which, unlike fragmented and routinized factory work, includes all aspects from conception through execution and even distribution. A (shortened) description of the stages of production of the "Vietnam curriculum" illustrates the processes involved.

First of all, there is an anonymous inspiration, then a collective beginning:

There was this idea that somebody should develop a Vietnam curriculum. And there was this little box for people's ideas. And in this box were ideas submitted by (five people), so the five of us decided to meet. And we became a little ad hoc Vietnam curriculum group, and began to develop high school curriculum together.

At every stage, there are mechanical tasks: "And I would use all my time at the office typing this stuff up and running it off on their Xeroxes." But the project generates meaning in connection with its political aims. Even social relations are influenced by, and in turn, influence the ongoing work: "And we had formed something called 'the ———— teachers' group,' and it met at different people's houses, and it was wonderful. We often had thirty or forty people there. So we would have these wonderful discussions on everything from discipline to how you teach Vietnam in the classroom."

The ever-present tensions between wage labor and political action,

implementation and creation, are played out here. When the narrator
felt that her substitute teaching job was unbearable, she "almost quit,"

> but the only reason I didn't, actually, was the work on the Viet-
> nam curriculum, because we had decided, somewhere in the
> middle of this, that we were gonna stick with this thing, that
> we were gonna try to publish something, and we were gonna
> get it out to people no matter what. And you can't write curric-
> ulum if you're not a teacher!

Later, however, this woman was able to work on production and
distribution full time, because, "by early spring we had raised some
money. We went to various rich people around, and this was like the
first Vietnam curriculum being worked on, and we were able to raise
money." She laughs when she remembers, "I was living on practically
nothing in those days. I considered two thousand dollars a year enough.
To live on! And, so I was able to spend all my time working on this."

The Partisan Artisan

Judging from her enthusiastic description, this woman, and those with
whom she works, value their own productivity highly, and are proud
of the intensity of their labor, but only when they are involved in the
production of political understanding. For this reason, and because the
women in this group also make a point of emphasizing both the mental
and the manual aspects of their work, I call the metaphorical identity
which they have created "the partisan artisan."

> We basically used a lot of stuff from the Times, and other news-
> papers as our sources, and just tried to write really provocative
> lessons around these things. It was a lot of work, you know,
> and we put in a tremendous amount of work into this thing.
> The first version of this we typed and mimeographed the entire
> thing and assembled ourselves.

This woman's description of the last stage of this project is reminis-
cent of Hobsbaum's (1984) observations on "political shoemakers,"
for, as unmarried journey-persons, these "worker-intellectuals and
ideologists" are easily able to travel from place to place, spreading
radical ideas.

So I spent the fall of '68, it was a *wonderful,* wonderful fall for me, travelling around to different schools, all over the area, with the Vietnam curriculum, and meeting with groups of teachers and trying to convince them that it was not too controversial to teach about the war.

And it was *really* organizing work. It was really solid organizing work in a way I don't think I've done since. Two of us did it and I think we went to several hundred schools. We had a network by then, because of our teachers' group. We had meetings, with anywhere from ten to fifteen or twenty teachers. Totally unofficial, unsupported by anybody within the school system. It was just teacher to teacher.

In this and other instances, the educational work of the political "atelier" (artisans' workshop) overlaps, but does not coincide with, employment in a school. Schools, with their standardized curriculum, managerial organization, and so forth, are more like "usines" (factories) than workshops. Membership in the partisan artisans' association is voluntary and temporary, based on a commitment to the cooperative development of a particular political curriculum. And, of course, the artisans are not paid for this extra work.

The partisan artisans' networks also do not coincide with conventional workers' organizations, unions. In these narratives, unions are regularly criticized for their conservative leadership, their narrow economic agendas, and their neglect of curricular issues. One woman remarks:

I had a few friends who were high school teachers. And they never discussed high school teaching. They discussed union organizing in the high schools, they discussed efforts to change the status of teaching with union organizing, but they never discussed what went on in their classes, or problems of teaching kids, or organization of schools, no issues having to do with the educational rights of teachers. Or of kids, ever. I mean, if they thought about them, which they may have, it was never something they discoursed about.

The Student as Political Apprentice

During a teachers' strike, the children she taught were a major concern for this same woman. She took the earliest picketing shift, and then met her students on a street corner. Throughout the strike, she spent the entire day with the children, visiting public parks and museums. "We had a wonderful time," she remembers; at the end of the strike, she really regretted the loss of this "informal" arrangement.

When the women in this group talk about their relationships with their students, what is described is more than simple political advocacy; the predicaments of these children and adolescents become an integral part of the teachers' own identities and perspectives. Only an inner-city school teacher could comment: "We also would do just straight-out curriculum stuff like this. Little wonderful science ideas for elementary classrooms. *Cockroaches.* I loved this magazine."

On a more serious note, this same woman pointed out an article she had written about George Jackson:[25]

> I was writing a lot. And enjoying it a lot. I had this teacher voice, and, I wrote this piece that meant a lot to me. I wrote a piece about George Jackson. What I tried to do in this article was connect up the life of George Jackson just in terms that teachers would understand. So I wrote it from a teacher's point of view of reading his memoirs and saying, "Listen, you've all had George Jacksons in your classroom." So that was what that piece is. It was really exciting. He, for some reason, he really meant a lot to me.

The life of this teacher has been permanently transformed through her interactions with black children. In the voice of George Jackson, she hears their voices, asking her political questions. In the article, she writes:

> What real life alternatives could we offer a young George Jackson? What alternatives would we want to offer him? If I had known George Jackson at the age of fifteen, would I have tried to draw him into Upward Bound, or the Black Panthers? Would either have averted the inevitability of prison?
>   The questions go on and on. You wonder if it's worth the constant hassle. But somehow, the immensity of George Jackson's efforts to educate himself, to learn in prison what he failed to learn at home and in school, reconfirms the importance of continuing the struggle.

And all these thoughts makes the clichéd truth that children are influenced by their teachers carry a new and very heavy weight. For if the teacher is a partisan artisan, then the student is a political apprentice.

I Answer With My Life

When this woman, together with a small group of politically compatible teacher friends, wanted to develop a curriculum on "social identity" ("what we really meant was *class*), a foundation grant allowed them to create a summer program.

> That was a wonderful experience. 'Cause I got a chance to teach, in a way I hadn't been able to do as a sub, with a consistent group of kids over the whole summer and I was with friends. The five of us team-taught. Clusters of kids. Everyone was supposed to develop materials on their own neighborhood. And we did a lot of travelling to each other's neighborhoods, and finding out about race and class, and it was really exciting!

This was the perfect curriculum making process: a team of teacher-artisans working cooperatively, in conjunction with their apprentice students, to investigate the social and political dynamics of their immediate environment. Eventually this project developed into "an actual curriculum for kids where they'd look at their own schooling," which this woman "ended up using in later years when I was doing the (alternative) school."

> Kids were coming in who had had *terrible* schooling experiences, who felt terrible about themselves because of it. And it was this incredible opportunity for them to look back at what they'd gone through and to name it. That they had been victimized basically, and it was not that they were stupid and that they were fuck-offs and all that kind of stuff. So we developed a course, and we taught it every year to all incoming students.

Of course, not every student chooses to be part of the political project; the article on George Jackson makes that very clear. But the bond between the teacher and those willing to join in the collective political learning process is very strong. This same woman was forced to resign a public school teaching job because of the ways in which she was identified with her politically active students.

> Things started to heat up for me a lot because I got involved in the Women's Movement. And I started to run a women's group at ——— high school, which ended up getting me in a fair amount of hot water. Because the women's group that I ran decided to have a women's day, and they invited people from gay liberation. And a couple of men came who totally

102

freaked out some of the kids, to a point where a complaint was filed against me, and I was censured in my record.

At the same time, I was very involved with the student group that called a student strike around the Kent state stuff. So, when, you know, fifteen students were standing up on a balcony in the middle of the schoolyard, I was the one teacher up there with them. So, that, plus the women's day, did me in.

In spite of disastrous consequences at the time, this woman does not regret her actions.

I still have kids, who are in their thirties now, from that time, who I am in contact with, or people who look me up. One girl found me ten years later, and said she wanted me to know that it was because of me that she'd become a feminist and all this stuff. She said that my class and the politics that I'd presented had made this big impression on her.

In this, and other descriptions of teachers' involvement in curriculum development projects, a perceived need for students to develop political understanding is a major motivating factor; the successful accomplishment of that goal, a cause for personal delight.

In a more recent example, a teacher "put (her) political energy into trying to develop a curriculum" which would explain governmental funding cuts within a wider social and political context.

It was not surprising that the quality of teaching and public services, et cetera, went way down. Whereas, at the same time, spending on the military was going way up. So we tried to make these connections.

The purpose of writing it was to reach urban kids. At the time a lot of anti-nuke curricula were coming out. But it was mostly for suburban kids, and it was mostly around the nuclear issue. And we wanted it to be much broader than that. So we wrote this thing. And we thought that it would have its best impact on urban kids, because they were the ones who were suffering the most from the impacts of all the cutbacks.

The influence of this project on her own ESL students was far-reaching and dramatic. At the beginning of the year, she recalls, her students were very reticent: "Every homeroom was supposed to send a representative to the student council. And I couldn't get the kids to go. I couldn't get them to elect anyone. They were too scared, their English wasn't good enough, et cetera." After she taught the curriculum, however,

> they were easily making connections between why their city schools were suffering so much and the suburbs were not suffering. They were making all the connections. They called up the president of the school committee themselves and asked for a meeting time with her. And they asked her questions like, "Why are you endorsing all these cutbacks?" and "Isn't there some way that we could get out of this?"; "Isn't there somewhere we could get the money?"

"So after they were able to do all that," she observes, "they *certainly* could join the student council. And they were all clamoring to join the student council."

And the effects just continued to grow. "There was a leadership conference, and they were *dying* to go to that. And they were really bowled over. They had never *been* to such a thing."

> And that was also the year of the big peace rally. And we took a whole busload of kids down. That was their first time ever being in a big American city. And a lot of these kids come from the mountains of Santa Domingo and Costa Rico and Guatemala and El Salvador. They had never seen a city like that. That was a major, major experience for them.

She was amazed by the process she had set into motion: "I never saw the kids open up the way they did, because they were really segregated off into their own little department in the school, in their own little wing, and now they were out there. They wanted to get to meet everybody. And it was really great. It was wonderful."

At this point in time, she was laid off (because of the spending cuts!) then rehired, but transferred to another school. When she went back to visit her former students, "they all came clamoring up to me, and the first thing they said was "——— is running for mayor and we wanna work on his campaign. How, what can we do?" And that was because they had met him over the summer."

Making a complete circle, the apprentice-students of the artisan-teacher had become activists themselves. "These kids were really on the ball. And I thought to myself, "god," 'cause the curriculum was very activity-oriented. It was also very empowering. It was really a lot of fun."

Teachers Working for Social Change

"There isn't a good term for those of us," explains one woman in this group, "who are still motivated by the civil rights agenda!" Recruited at a time when teachers were scarce, and schools were a central project of a movement in ascendancy, these women continue to work in education, building progressive enclaves with the state system with the support of their constituency of parents and students. And they have accomplished material restructurings of schooling: one of them participated in the "creation" of a new junior high school; another was the founder of a group of alternative open education schools within a large school system; one of them was an original organizer of an alternative high school which achieved regular accreditation from the board of education; one of them succeeded in having a progressive curriculum officially adopted throughout a whole city system.

It is not only in the articulation of a progressive discourse through their life history narratives, therefore, that these women can be called authors. Their stories tell how teachers, working in cooperative political groups, can change the meaning of education for those with whom they come in contact. This is the creation of social text at a very fundamental level.

5

A Signifying Discourse of Black Women Teachers Working for Social Change

Introduction

From the very beginning of my project, I was determined to include black[26] women teachers' narratives. Yet the confusion I felt between my initial intentions and my final analysis, a period of more than five years, demands documentation, for it reveals the unexpected ways in which "I became acutely aware of my own subjectivity" (Peshkin, 1988: 17).

I did not come academically unprepared to this particular part of my research. I had made a deliberate and intensive study of ethnicity and race in education; I had written about the philosophical presuppositions and policy implications of various definitions of ethnicity and race; and I certainly understood the "social construction" of ethnicity and race on a theoretical level.[27]

The difficulty which I experienced in conceptualizing the narratives of black teachers must be explained in terms of the extraordinary power and persistence of my own racial interpellation. In contrast to my belief that I could elicit and analyze the narratives of Catholic women religious and Jewish women of the New Left (even though I was neither a nun nor Jewish), throughout my study of black women teachers I have been troubled by the fear that I would not be told or could not understand the life stories of this group because I am white.

That I left the interpretation of these narratives until last, therefore, is not coincidental. Then, when I was unable to easily perceive significant patterns in the narratives of black women teachers, I forgot the amount of time and effort which it had taken to understand the logic of the other groups's stories, and began to attribute failure to a combination of my white identity and technical inadequacy.

I had collected very long and very rich life histories from two women with whom I was already acquainted. One woman (introduced by a third party) lent me a tape she had made with another white interviewer. Both she and a fourth woman (contacted through a chain of mutual acquaintances) asked me not to use my tape recorder, but did not object when I took notes. I did not feel that these were personally hostile encounters, but I was disturbed, for while I could sympathize with the rejection of an eavesdropping machine, I did feel that I was left with an uneven record of their stories.

What I never doubted was the value of even one of the remarkable phrases which I held in trust. Whenever I quoted from these narratives (Casey, 1987; 1988b; 1988c; 1989; 1990a), the audience was enthralled. However tentative my presentations were, the women's own words rang out loud and clear, creating significance within the virtual vacuum of research on black teachers. I knew of no other studies focusing on contemporary black women teachers when I began the research, and I was continually provoked by such neglect to persist in my own work.

As the public debate on education developed in the eighties, some policy analysts did take notice of black teachers, projecting a "shortage" of "minority" teachers (for instance, Graham, 1987; Tewel and Trubowitz, 1987; Irvine, 1988; Murnane and Schwinden, 1988; Kemple, 1989; Perkins, 1989). Here, ironically, the administrative gaze focuses on future absence, not present presence; black teachers become significant as negative numbers. Like many other articles concerned with teacher attrition, these pieces confidently construct public policy recommendations without ever soliciting teachers' testimonies (Casey, 1992). Yet the extent of this instrumental view of black teachers greatly exceeds the usual disdain for white teachers' interpretations, because it also encompasses a process of racial objectification.

It is now clear to me that the development of progressive scholarship in the eighties was a collective endeavor to which I contributed and from which I benefitted. It was in the process of that dialogue that I was eventually able to perceive patterns where I had originally seen only a ragged collection of fragments; I was finally able to shift from using illustrative quotations to describing the generative matrix of a coherent discourse.

Conversations with my colleagues, Susan Laird and Jan Jipson, together with Marianne Hirsch's (1989) book, *The Mother/Daughter Plot,* inspired a paper on teacher-as-mother (Casey, 1990a), which gave me my first real insight into the central controlling metaphor of the black women teachers' narratives. Then, in 1990 (at the same American Educational Research Association meeting where I was to present that paper, a symposium entitled *Capturing the Black Teacher's Voice*[28] proved to be an extraordinary event; here I found black scholars attentive to the interpretations of black teachers, and here I realized how much I already understood about these stories. When two of the speakers, Michele Foster and Annette Henry, attended the reading of my paper and commented that I might have been reading from one of their transcripts, I was finally able to lay to rest the notion that my collection of narratives had somehow been compromised. What I now needed to figure out was why the black women who produced the life histories were less concerned with my racial identity as I was myself.

I am now dumbfounded by the fact that I had apparently "forgotten" that three out of the four women knew that my daughter was black. So, as I listened to their stories, I was being addressed as a person who understood at least some of the black cultural repertoire, someone who knew some of the passwords. I now believe that it was precisely as a mother of a black child that I was in an exceptionally good position to call forth the metaphor of the outraged mother, described below.

Because my research project was explicitly defined in terms of progressive political activism, I was also addressed as someone who stood on common ideological ground. There are several passages in the narratives which clearly acknowledge this relationship. One woman comments on seeing my daughter at an anti-apartheid rally in one part of her story, then makes political distinctions among local black leaders in another:

> I have found occasions where it was difficult to deal with
> blacks who were coming from a different political agenda, as
> well as a different economic agenda and a different self-serving
> agenda.—You do get on the Urban League Board, oh gosh, I'm
> gonna say this, right into the tape, a lot of bourgeois niggers!
> Oh! At least that's the in-house word, and that's what we call
> them. On the one hand, you know, very, very committed, but
> on the other hand, very, very self-serving, you know, and you
> have to come to grips with that, too.

The speaker dares to use a private black phrase within the public integrated context which I represent because she believes that we share concerns about class and gender as well as about race.[29]

But this quotation must be interpreted not only in connection with the particular social relations of research which gave it shape; it must also be understood as part of the larger complicated relationship between black and white discourses in America. Remarking on the intricacies of this cultural dialogue, Gates (1989: 30) observes that the "gap of difference between what we see among and for ourselves and what we choose to tell in (a white, or integrated) public discourse has been remarkably complex in our tradition." The corresponding complexity with which certain critics explicated and defined the black literary tradition in the eighties profoundly influenced the final phases of my analysis; it is difficult for me to imagine that I could have achieved much depth without responding to this material.

My aim has always been to present the narratives of black women with the same attention to their integrity which characterizes my studies of other groups of teachers. Gates' (1988: xix) articulate description of his intentions speaks of what I hope to achieve:

> My desire has been to allow the black tradition to speak for itself about its nature and various functions, rather than to read it, or analyze it, in terms of—theories borrowed whole from other traditions, appropriated from without.

while Braxton's (1989: 6) observations recognize the difficulties which I have encountered:

> This is not to assert that those born outside the "magic circle" of the black and female "world of love and ritual" are forever locked outside the text. For the text is accessible to whoever would first establish its proper cultural context, thus gaining access to a sphere of privileged (and valuable) knowledge.—The critic who is *not* a black woman must simply work harder to see the black woman at the center of her own—experience.

Interpretive Questions; Signifying Answers

The challenge, in Gates's (1988: 258) words, is "to turn away from, to step outside the white hermeneutical circle and into the black." For black readers, this may consist of self-consciously shifting into a particular code; for white, entering an unfamiliar system of meanings;

in either case, the exegete needs to place a black narrator's text within a black cultural context.

When I began to read these women's life histories together with creative and critical works by other black authors, powerful common patterns began to emerge, suggesting that it was my analytic schema (not the stories) which had been fragmentary and inadequate. In my final analysis, the black women teachers can be seen, like black writers who "critique other black texts as an act of rhetorical self-definition" (Gates, 1984a: 290), creating their identities in active dialogue with (vernacular and literary versions of) black culture.

But simultaneously, analysis of these narratives demands attention to (various versions of) white culture within which these women also participate, albeit in a subordinated position. For white and black discourses in this country "do not exclude, but rather intersect with each other" (Bakhtin, 1981: 291) in specific and peculiar ways. Like the social groups that generate them, these sets of explanations are characterized by asymmetrical power relations; inside the dominant white text, black women appear as silenced and inferior figures.

The search for a coherent discourse must begin by rejecting the assumption that black women teachers necessarily have anything in common,[30] for the homogeneity routinely attributed to black women is, in fact, created by a white gaze which perceives her as "a mute, visible object" (Johnson, 1989: 44). The "complexities of (her) experience" have been "subsume(d) into a tractable sign" which "void(s) the possibility of meaning within the 'blackened' shell of selfhood" (Benston, 1989: 156–157). To analyze the discourse of black women, therefore, we must recognize the ways in which their narratives challenge the dominant white meanings which have always already been constructed around their personal, work, and social relations.

Referring to black discourse in general, Gates (1987: 37) remarks in this regard: "our history often turns on a tension, a dialectic, between the private perceptions of the individual and the white public perceptions of that same individual." Like other versions of black narrative, these life histories speak out of a double consciousness: "It is a peculiar sensation—this sense of always looking at one's self through the eyes of others, of measuring one's soul by the tape of a world that looks on in amused contempt and pity (DuBois, 1965: 214–215); "I have been called one thing and then another, while no one really wished to hear what I called myself" (Ellison, 1972: 560).

So (re)interpretation is a central imperative of these life histories. As black women, as teachers, as political activists, and as authors of their own lives, these narrators pride themselves upon being guerrilla fighters in a semiotic war. Avoiding direct confrontation, they cast an innocent smile to signal repudiation, turn a contended phrase to indicate defiance. If you are not alert to their covert intentions, you could easily miss these twists of meaning.

This oblique intersection of black and white meanings within black narrative is a specifically black form of (re)interpretation called "signifyin(g)" (Gates, 1988: xxiv):

> Free of the white person's gaze, black people created their own unique vernacular structures and relished in the double play that these forms bore to white forms. Repetition and revision are fundamental to black artistic forms. . . . Signifyin(g) . . . *is* repetition and revision, or repetition with a signal difference. Whatever is black about black American literature is to be found in this identifiable black Signifyin(g) difference.

Alternatively, and with particular reference to black women's expression, Wall (1989: 10–11) names this mode of interpretation "changing words" (after a phrase which Zora Heale Hurston appropriated from the vernacular), or simply "talking back."

Fundamental questions of interpretation are raised when black speakers respond to attempted impositions of white versions of reality by manipulating the import of the original utterance. Take, for example, Winson Hudson's account (in Crawford, 1990: 17) of her attempts to register to vote. Here signifying is both the form and content of the story:

> We had to fill out an application and had to read and interpret the Mississippi constitution, section 44. You had to read and interpret it to the *t*. It was little bitty writing and you had to copy it and interpret it and I mean you couldn't leave an *i* undotted. . . . My husband was registered; I guess they thought he was white. You couldn't tell him from a white man. . . . We finally got the justice department in here and they went over to the courthouse and they asked about me and my sister and the clerk said they can register. We went back over there and filled out the application. (The registrar) gave me the same section 44 of the Mississippi constitution. When it got to the part that said interpret, I wrote that *it said what it meant and it meant what it said*. The clerk said, "Winson, you passed." (emphasis added).

The phrase, it said what it meant and it meant what it said, mocks the very notion of "correct" meaning, and yet, ironically, it is accepted as such. The interchange can only be understood within the context of racial relations in Mississippi, but at the same time, the significance of race is radically undermined when the same white clerk refuses to register a black woman, misinterprets her husband's color, and finally, under duress, allows her, in an unconscious pun, to "pass."

Like the narrators to be presented, this speaker symbolically and materially subverts her received identity; like the narratives to be discussed, this anecdote contains corresponding motifs of disguise, disclosure, reversal, and sass. Chronicled in this account is the same racial contestation over language which reverberates in the featured life histories of black women teachers, and throughout black tradition. To acknowledge the systematic subjugation of black constructions of meaning in this country (through the annihilation of African languages; compulsory illiteracy laws; literacy tests for voting; nonexistent, inadequately financed, or Eurocentric schooling) is to understand why interpretation continues to be a major terrain of racial struggle, and why the slave narrative tradition persists as a matrix of black expression.

Identity as Reversal

We are sitting in her classroom, the tape recorder on the table between us; she consults her notes, and then, to my astonishment, she begins talking about picking cotton.

As a child, I always worked. My earliest memories of working in the field, you know, had to do with visiting my grandmother, and my grandmother making me a cotton sack to go out into the fields. I think I was like six years old, and at that point it was pretty much child's play, but within a few years, it took on a really serious note, and, you know, my father counted every pound. So from the time I was like eight or nine years old on, I would spend afternoons after school and all day Saturday, either working my daddy's cotton farm, or his pea farm, or his potato farm, or his cucumber farm, depending on the season of the year, doing either gathering crops or nourishing the crops, or we called it, cotton cropping and cotton hoeing.

I Answer With My Life

More than just an account of her own childhood poverty, this story calls to mind millions of African children held in bondage: "I was born a slave; but I never knew it till six years of happy childhood had passed away" (Brent, 1973: 3); it evokes the memory of Fannie Lou Hamer (in Wright, 1968: 1–2).

> One day when I was about six, I was playing beside a gravel road . . . and the landowner came and asked me could I pick cotton, I told him I didn't know. He told me if I picked thirty pounds of cotton that week that they would carry me to a commissionary store . . . on the plantation(s) . . . that Saturday, and I would get Cracker Jacks and Daddy-Wide Legs . . . and cherries. . . . And this was things that we had never had. I picked thirty pounds that week. . . . Then the next week I was tasked to sixty because what he was really doing, was trapping me into work. . . . I . . . had to pick more and more. By the time I was thirteen years old, I was picking three and four hundred (pounds).

By grounding her narrative in the cotton fields of Mississippi, the speaker claims a timeless connection to the slave experience. The person that I thought I knew—the articulate teacher, the militant activist, the sophisticated woman who, by her own description, wears size five to six, and enjoys "flashy dresses" and "flashy shoes"—is also a "daughter of captivity."[31] While this may not be an identity which the white world ordinarily recognizes, it is the self from which her authorship proceeds.

The tension provoked by the apparent contrast between this individual teacher's past and present conditions moves the listener to recognize the continuity of oppression throughout the history of black presence in this country. But the purpose of this life history is not simply to document victimization; quite the reverse, the object is to wage and to win an interpretive war.

So no stereotypical assumption is left unopposed as the narrator repeatedly challenges the listener: you do not know who I am. You think I am a middle-class teacher . . . but I picked cotton as a child. I worked in the fields . . . but my father owned the land.

> My father was a farmer who really enjoyed farming. Most of all, I believe he enjoyed farming his own land. He took as much pride in farming his land, I think, as he did in his family. The land was extremely important because many people in our

community were sharecroppers. And for as long as I remembered, and I think for as long as my father remembered, since he was a small boy, the ———— had always owned their land.

Under these circumstances, agricultural labor becomes the very inversion of servitude:[32]

> To own one's own land gave one a certain amount of independence. A lot of that independence was, of course, psychological, but psychological independence that was based on reality, and that is, if you owned your own land, you *could,* to more of a degree than those that did not, control your own destiny. And my father was a very fearless believer in controlling as much of his destiny as he could.
>
> He understood that in the very real world, the white man was in control, and he did have ultimate power. But my father's attitude was, "He's not here." You know. "I don't have him ordering my children around. I don't have him looking me in the face and telling me what to do."

In this family's story, then, it is white employers, not black workers, who appear as caricatures: "My father refused to work any job where he'd have to punch a clock, and have Mr. Charlie, as we called him, tell him what to do on an ongoing basis"; "We would work *with* him, just be in the fields and so forth, but not in Miss Ann's kitchen."

An adverse consequence of this "fearless pride," she remembers, was that "we were very poor." "There were times when economically it was very, very difficult." "His not taking that day-job with the white boss really did deny us a lot of things economically."

> For example, a decent home to live in. We lived in this . . . it was like a three-room shack. Really, a shack. You would wake up in the morning when someone would see the sun rise, and you would look down at night and you could hear the chickens underneath the house, or if they fluttered, the dust would come up through the cracks in this floor.

Of course, this description aims to document material deprivation in the rural South of the narrator's childhood. But, at least as importantly, the shabby shack, like the child in the cotton field, stands to mock the reader who, like the tourist speeding through Mississippi, would catch a glimpse, and drive on by, only to meet a roadblock just up the road.

115

Stop, says the storyteller, and turn around; you have misinterpreted the significance of these scenes. "Growing up in an environment that was so racist and growing up in an environment that was so *poor*, economically, you had to be rich in something. And we were rich in love. We were rich in ownership, and we were rich in caring."

When she was young, she admits, she herself did not fully understand her father. "He was very much a patriarch, an iron-handed man, in controlling his family, but definitely in terms of controlling the girls in his family." As an adolescent, she was "opposed to being protected," "to not being given freedoms" that she saw men around her being given. "I wanted to be myself and I wanted to be me, and I didn't want to be controlled." In a general sense she now sees that, "when you have a family of nine children and you're living on a shoestring budget, and, you know, you've got all this racism surrounding you, there's not a lot of room for compromise and negotiation; you either take charge or you die."

But, more specifically, she has become conscious of her particular vulnerability as a black *female* child. Like the other stories in this group, this is a distinctly "Afra-American" narrative.[33]

> My father never really, nor my mother, you know, would sit down and have a real, confrontative conversation with us about . . . facing the white man's attitude towards black women, but it was always implicit in most of the things that he did and said. In terms of his protecting us. For example, never allowing his girls to go to work for white people unless he was there. We spent many a day working in the field of white men, but my father never sent us unless he was there. I heard him utter on several occasions that "a girl of mine" would never work in a kitchen of some white man. And, during those days I guess I didn't really understand why. I didn't. I thought, well, it'd be a good way to make three dollars, you know. But my father would never hear of it.

Thus her parents develop and maintain the integrity of their child's self-identity by revising and reversing the historical relationship between the white male master and the black female slave child. In this version, worker control over the conditions of labor is more important than economic gain; the independence of distance is preferable to the intimacy of proximity; manual agricultural labor in the fields is superior to menial domestic labor in the house. The hierarchy of plantation privilege is overturned, and *this* little black girl will not become another

"Mammy," cooking white people's meals, scrubbing white people's floors, and minding white people's children.

Even while she produces a more sympathetic interpretation of her father's behavior, the narrator cannot resist a purely "womanist" boast in her narrative, simultaneously dismissing stereotypes of the weak woman and the lazy black worker.

> But I was always into doing the best I could of whatever job was available. And I could pick as much cotton as my father. My brothers would be somewhere back in the back, and pretty soon, it got to the point where I could pick *more* cotton than my father. And I was a two hundred fifty pound picker. And that's a lot of cotton for someone to pick in one day's time. And my mother was also that kind of hard worker. She would never stop until it was done.

But the final ironic twist to the whole cotton-picking story is that the money which the family jointly earns through manual labor is spent on the children's higher education.

> I remember sitting around the table on a Saturday night after we had worked hard all day, after we would get home from school we'd go and work, and counting our pennies and putting 'em in the middle of the table, and my mother would take that money and send it to my brother to pay the month's room and board, or to buy a book that he needed. And it was incidents like that that really pointed out the closeness of the family, and how we really needed each other.
>
> When I look back on that experience and when I think of my mother and father getting in gear to send my brother to college, and they didn't have a damn penny to do it with! I just kind of laugh, you know. It's just hysterical. I mean, they were getting ready to, you know, mortgage the cow, and sell a hog, and sell a few chickens, and sell the first bale of cotton, and make sure that that went to pay the first semester's tuition, and all kinds of little, real magic tricks.

Identity as Disguise

Parallel motifs appear in the childhood memories of a woman who grew up in New Orleans. Her family also refused to let her do domestic work:

I Answer With My Life

This is why I don't cook to this date. They wouldn't let me cook. In fact, they cooked so well there was no need for me to cook; I just sat there and appreciated all this great cooking.

The thing that I remember bothered me was they wouldn't let me baby-sit. Other girls were getting baby-sitting jobs and the best babysitting jobs *were* with white families. They would *not* let me do that at all! Then other girls would work behind the drug store counter, which was segregated, and they just would not let me do that.

I was not to serve whites in any way, and I didn't! But I was real upset, you know. Everyone else had some pocket money, and I just didn't have a penny, but that was one thing my family had going.

Instead they encourage her intellectual achievements:

When I was three years old, my mother was gonna take me to the river. And we were going to visit some big ship that had come in. And I kept saying, "I'm going to see the big boat." And she said, "No, a big boat is called a ship." And I kept referring to it as a big boat. So, in desperation, she got a piece of paper, and she wrote, "This is water." And she drew a wave. "This is a boat," and she drew it. "This is a ship." And something about the *this is* with a different word there, and *the,* and the diagram, I *immediately* read it.

And then I could read anything thereafter. It was just like . . . Oh! And I remember that *very* day. I read everything from then on. I don't know what method of teaching reading that is, but whatever it was, you know, it clicked. But it made me this early reader, which then all the neighbors and relatives took very seriously. And that determined what kind of person, I guess, I was going to be.

Here again, the adult speaker portrays her childhood self in two distinct dimensions: protected and nurtured within her black family; conspicuous and vulnerable on the white public landscape.

But, as this second narrator tells me her story, I am again confounded, this time because I hear someone who talks about being "black," yet I see someone who looks "white." Indeed, here is a woman who has regularly experienced the "special, strange feeling of being mistaken for who I wasn't." And, here is a storyteller who uses disguise and concealment, trickery and wit, "devices long important in the slave

118

narrative tradition" (Braxton, p. 29), to confuse her foes; disclosure and laughter to support her friends. The resulting life history is an extraordinarily complex and ironic (re)construction of the significance of race.

Clearly proud of the way in which her very existence confuses racial categorization, the narrator's disclosure of her origins is not so much a biological as a political description of how her family undermines the "stratified system" of race. She explains that her mother's mother (after whom she is named) came from a "tiny tribe" of Indians in Louisiana; her mother's father was an "obviously" black man. She remembers her mother's disdain for racial distinctions; in the Catholic church, "the whites were sitting in the front, and some of the better off, light-complexioned blacks were sitting next, the darker-complexioned blacks were sitting next, and the Indians were actually standing up! My mother thought that was stupid."

Her father's father was an English immigrant; her father's mother was a white Cajun woman; he was their first and only child. When his mother died, his father lived with a light-complexioned black Creole woman, and they had several children. The narrator's father, who "technically" was white, was then "raised black" with the other children. Consequently, she states, her father was "a very, very interesting person." "We were boycotting South African stuff back when I was a little girl, 'cause he knew every place in the world where there was something on racial stuff, because I think he felt in a strange position. He was militantly pro black, even though he was snow white!"

An antithesis of the stereotypical "tragic mulatta," this author construes her own racial ambiguity as radical (re)interpretive possibility. Because of her appearance, this woman explains, but also because of where she lived, she was a beloved child not only within her immediate family, but also in the whole neighborhood.

> I lived in a section of town that had a lot of immigrants. There were Greeks, and there were Italians, and there were Mexicans, a Mexican-Italian couple, a real cosmopolitan couple there. And these people didn't live any place else in town. And there were some Jewish people, shop owners and stuff.
>
> And we'd go up and down the street, we were treated grandly, my brother and I, because we actually looked like the various ones. The Greeks would treat us like Greeks, and they would give us a little apple or a little something, and they'd pat us on the head.
>
> Now they actually knew who we were. They knew who my

mother was and they knew the whole scene. But they still didn't care. And when somebody treats you that way, well, you feel good, you know. And so we were just cute little kids, and then, of course, the blacks treated us friendly, and then all those whites.

But this life history is much more complicated than a simple celebration of racial indeterminacy. In the act of articulating her own identity, this speaker acknowledges real racist dangers, but accentuates their contingent condition, and then, sabotages their supposed significance.

In this account of growing up in New Orleans, the child learns to recognize, deconstruct, and reinterpret social signs, a process very clearly depicted in a series of stories about the public transportation system. As a three-year-old, this woman recounts, she demanded to know the meaning of a sign on the tram:

> When I was a little girl, the very day I learned to read, I remember I asked my mother . . . I thought it was a headrest. Oh! She *told* me it was a headrest. I said, "I want to have that behind my head." So I could lean on it. And she said, "What? No, you can't."
>
> And I said, "Why can't I have a turn having the headrest?" And she just told me I couldn't ever have the headrest. And I thought that was the most unfair thing. And I remember reading, "For Colored Only." And then I didn't, I still didn't know quite what all that was, you know! But people find out soon enough.

So she pictures herself as a kind of baby semiotician who can identify injustice even when her protective mother deliberately misinterprets a symbol of segregation.

As the narrator elaborates on the physical construction of the racial dividers, it is important to note how she stresses their mobility, as well as how she combines her explanation with a discussion of Mardi Gras, a time when they are temporarily inoperative.

> They weren't the huge kind of screens that they had in Alabama and Mississippi; these were just little wooden signs that were supported by little metal things which would stick in two little holes.
>
> And you could move it. So that conceivably if a whole bus-full of blacks got on, and there were hardly any whites, you

could move it up to the *very* front. Only the long facing seats, you know, you could move it right to there. And if you were white, you could move it all the way back except for the back seat.

Now what whites could do that blacks couldn't is that they could move it. Some real prejudiced types could get on, and move it all the way back, and no black could sit down. Let's say a whole busfull of blacks got on, then they could not sit in front of that guy. Now you could ask him to. Sometimes folks would fall asleep and you'd nudge him and say, "Would you, could you, move?" And if they said "No," well, then, you had to stand. And of course, a black *never* could do that. Boy, oh, boy, they had to be sure that they were never keeping a white from being seated.

Well, on Mardi Gras day, all of these things left. And people sat any kind of way they wanted to. And not just for Mardi Gras, that whole week.

Of course, as she and her listeners now know, the conditional nature of these barriers was ultimately demonstrated with their removal as a result of civil rights struggles.

Even before the adults' bus boycotts began, the narrator remembers, rebellious adolescents, humiliated by the fact that "you had to face the screen; if you were colored, that wording faced you," conducted a guerilla campaign. In this hide-and-seek game of identity politics, their tactics consisted of quite literally deconstructing the system of signs.

I remember when I was a teenager, as kids got, you know, more to figuring it out, especially the fellas, it was really hard for them to sit behind it. And, at a certain point we were living temporarily way across town. And my friends would come to visit me from uptown. And the boys, my boyfriends, would steal . . . the sign. They would jump up, they would steal the sign, and *run* out the back door, and then they'd run for all their life, and they'd get to my house, and then have these things. (Laughs)

And I'd put it under my bed! And I had *quite* a collection under my bed. And when I went away to college, my mother threw them away. I came home, and that's what I *really* wanted. I wanted to take one to show people what this thing was like. And she always thought, somebody's gonna come in one time and *find* these things. It was dangerous, what we were doing, but!

Adolescent dread of public indignity appears in another streetcar story; here the narrator defends her integrity as a young black woman by playing a kind of racial peek-a-boo.

One of traditions on the streetcar was if a pretty girl got on the streetcar, the conductor would lead her to her seat and make a big production of it. I mean, a white girl. This was for white girls. Well! When I got on, and you have to imagine me one hundred pounds thinner, and I was considered kinda cute. I wore my hair long. At any rate, I had made an effort to look nice, one of my few efforts! And when he said, "*Hey,*" then I thought, "Oh, my effort paid off." You know, so I was really glad.

But then he started to lead me to my seat. And my seat, he assumed, was way up front in the street car. You gotta go way up, 'cause you enter through the colored section, and you had to walk forward. And I said. "Oh, this'll be fine." You know, I'm trying to sit. And he's just leading.

Now the blacks figure they know what's going on, you know! And they just can't wait to see this. So he put me down, and the screen was in back of me. That's the time I got to get the screen in back of me. Well, after he had gone back . . . I didn't wanna embarrass him . . . even though he was the cause of it, I got up, got the screen, moved it, and put it in front of me.

He comes up to tell me that I must be from another country, and I must not know that the screen does not go there; it goes behind me. I said, "No, it goes in front of me." And then, he looked at me, and he was *so* embarrassed. And the blacks fell down laughing, you know, that was *so* funny, you know!

Quite the opposite of equivocation, her game is a witty form of radical political defiance. Very politely, she maintains solidarity with other black passengers; very emphatically, she refuses to "pass."

But her (re)interpretive task is made more difficult by an existing historical script about "mulattas." Elsewhere in her narrative, she refers to "the not-so-distant past," when wealthy white men would look for their mistresses at "quadroon" and "octaroon" balls. So, she cannot simply choose to be "black."

One time I got on again, with the same guy, and then he knew exactly who I was, and he made a big production of seating me *in* the colored section. Still doing that same thing, and I didn't know *what* to make of that.

Because, another thing is a light-complexioned girl, I myself noticed that sometimes they were treated really as sex objects. By one and all. So I was determined, that I wasn't gonna fall into *that* case. I didn't want people to think I was his mistress, or there was any kind of familiarity going on here, you know! I mean, "Thank you *very* much," you know, I would put on my . . .! Oh! So I wound up with a very innocent. . . .

Oh, that was another thing. I *loved* men. But I always kept this real innocent . . . and even now, this still bothers my older daughter, that I'm a southern belle thing, but I just really ran this innocent southern belle thing into the ground! So I wouldn't be seen as a loose Creole girl.

While her initial response is consternation, and her strategy is to create confusion, there is no ambivalence in her final actions. The only narrator who speaks explicitly about the sexual dimension of race relations, this woman never forgets its sinister history:

I never envied being a male because I really felt that *they* were victims. Because the male black was the one who got lynched.—I had a cousin, who was one of these silly mulatto types, who was running around trying to get white girlfriends, and he got castrated and dumped into the bayou, and so we were told this tale, and my brother was told.

So, having revealed her "other-than-white" social identity, she then conceals her sexual self under a genteel "white" disguise. Refusing to be either black mammy or mulatta mistress, indeed, behaving like their direct opposite, the white southern belle, this narrator reverses what Christian (1985: 1) calls "the mythology of the South." By playing innocent, by acting fragile and helpless, she "addresse(s), use(s), trans-form(s), and subvert(s) the dominant ideological code" of "the cult of true womanhood" (Carby, 1987: 19–20).

Another black woman teacher's memory, "my father wanted me to be in a position to never lift anything heavier than a pen," pronounced with a smile, captures the same ironic appeal to a chivalric code. Not only does this father imagine a white lady's status for his black daughter; he also pictures literacy as its key component. To become an educated black woman is, for these families, to contradict the whole system of racist signification.

Education as Refutation

> The slave who was the first to read and the first to write was the first slave to run away. The correlation of freedom with literacy not only became the central trope of the slave narratives, but it also formed a mythical matrix out of which subsequent black narrative forms developed (Gates, 1987: 108).

In these narratives black children are taught black constructions of meaning by their families and communities; in that sense, they do not go to school to learn "how to read." Instead, in these stories, white-dominated educational institutions are *signified upon* by black students, parents, and teachers; they are (re)interpreted in such ways as to recuperate their purposes to the intentions of a black constituency. Central to this complex agenda of aspirations is the notion that knowledge is power; to be wise in "black" interpretation is essential to physical and psychic survival; but to succeed at studying "white" knowledge is to undo the system itself, to refute its (re)production of black inferiority materially and symbolically.

Knowing that these are life stories of black women who have become teachers, we can expect to hear about successful strategies for accomplishing this refutation. What these narratives also reveal are the personal consequences of racial struggles inside American schools following civil rights initiatives. In these particular accounts, young black women are not seen by others, nor do they see themselves, as *individuals* striving for academic achievement; within the institutions of education, they are interpellated as, and choose to present themselves as, representatives *of* and *for* their people.

So, within the context of these life histories, for a black mother in Boston to get a permit for her daughter to go out of the district to a "better (high) school" takes on more than individual significance. For the family of a wealthy black girl in New Orleans to refuse to send her to a neighborhood school, "in desperation" to "make" a small Methodist high school for black girls, has more than class significance.

For the narrator who was her friend and classmate, memories of attending that school are ironically triumphant. The black public high school which these girls were supposed to attend was an unusually well-funded part of a segregated system.

> Booker T. Washington was the show high school. They would put, funnel in lots of money, but it was a vocational school, and blacks really resented that. It was considered, we all gotta go to Booker T. Washington, and then graduate and go to Tuskegee or something, you know, that sort of thing. But they were really set up well. A beautiful building and everything. And it was *the* auditorium where you went for symphony concerts, where blacks went . . . for graduations. We graduated out of that auditorium.

In sharp contrast, even the wealthy black founders could not supply everything for the school they started. "We were pretty bad off in many departments like in the sciences, wow! That was awful," this woman recalls; we "took chemistry and physics with no lab." "For driver education, which was a state requirement, I made an A, and we didn't have a car! And I still wanna know how to drive!" Referring to her future area of specialization, she remembers that "even in music we didn't have any instruments to speak of."

> For band, we didn't have any of the double reeds, we didn't have tympanies. We were really good musicians, when it came to sight reading! And if it called for a tympani, we would yell, "Tympani!" When we needed double reeds, a friend would whip out his harmonica. And it would sound *just* like. . . . The quality would pierce through. And while he wouldn't sound *exactly* like an oboe, it had a quality. We could bring people to tears, you know, 'cause we really knew how we wanted it to sound!

In spite of the apparent deficiencies, by the time she finished high school, the speaker reports, "I had this really phenomenally high (test) score. So I had a choice of going to a lot of schools. They wanted me to go to Vassar . . . and Oberlin, I recall."

For another young woman determined to get the best education available, challenging prevailing racial arrangements made her feel highly conspicuous and very vulnerable.

> I really think that it was probably my decision, and my father's decision, when I was sixteen years old, to go to the integrated

schools in Mississippi. There are several reasons why I say that, and one is that it was a very . . . *brave* thing to do. Maybe I didn't even realize it at the time. I think I did though. Because at any point we could have been killed.

We were brought into that school on a segregated bus with only a white bus driver, and there were like eight black kids, and we were going across . . . seven to eight miles from the black school. And the Ku Klux Klan was kinda treacherous in those days. You know, they didn't take any shit!

Nevertheless, inside the school, she defended herself against the physical and psychological abuse of white students, and protested white administrators' definition of her presence. Employing white (national-northern) criteria against white (local-southern) policies, she raised fundamental interpretive questions about desegregation.

When we arrived at the school, we were, you know, spat upon, and names were yelled at us, and there were racial fights, and I almost got kicked out of school for fighting. I mean, I never took "no" for an answer when I was there. I was always questioning, and, you know, I wrote to the Justice Department, and had them come to investigate. Yeah! To investigate racism in the school. I mean, they had a separate study hall for the black students, they had a separate bathroom that we had to go to, and we had to sit at a separate table in the cafeteria. And so it was . . . real hell.

Listening to the narrator's report of the subsequent confrontation, it is important to note the exact words which the white principal uses, and the particular way which the young black woman responds.

And so I had the Justice Department come out to investigate, and the principal didn't like *that* too well, you know, and she says, "———, your great white fathers were out here today. I guess you saw them." And I says, "Well, I saw them." "Well, we can no longer make you sit at a certain table in the cafeteria, and you won't have your little study hall down there to play around in. Now we're gonna put you in there with the rest of the white children." I said, "Well, you know, I guess the good comes with the bad," because we actually liked that study hall!

The implications of this interchange are complex. Is the principal evoking a Native American stereotype to mock the (supposed) advantages of being a "minority" child? In that case, it is, at very least, a racist remark. But what does the key phrase "your great white fathers" (who are, presumably, from the great White House) mean if it is understood within the historical context of race and gender relations in Mississippi?

For a sixteen-year-old black woman to evoke an adult white male legal code is, in this slur, to breach the "biological" boundaries of gender and of race, to claim privilege which can never be "rightfully" hers, to commit an "illegitimate" act of self-revision. For the white female principal to mock her black female student's claim with such a phrase is also, in my interpretation, to implicate this (relatively light-complexioned) girl in a sordid version of sexual relations under slavery.

So challenged for her signifying act, the student "talks back" (Wall, pp. 10–11). Like her slave sisters before her, she answers her social superior (a vestigial white plantation mistress?) impudently and disrespectfully. Returning "a portion of the poison the master has offered her," she resorts to "sass" as a "weapon of (verbal) self-defense" (Braxton, p. 31). And her message? When it comes to education, she can bear passing insults for small victories, so that eventually she will be able to free herself and her people through her intellectual prowess.

The Genealogy of an Organic Intellectual[34]

Contrary to the white principal's insinuations, it is a *black* father who stands behind this young woman's determined activism, and one of her main intentions as an adult narrator is to defend him. Not only does she contradict one white person's indirect insult; she also repudiates the generalized white disdain for black men and black families which it implies. By recording her father's story ("and when I say my father, I'm speaking of my father and my mother; they were both that way," she explains) this women joins with other black authors in composing what Benston (p. 152) describes as "one vast genealogical poem which attempts to restore continuity to the ruptures—imposed by the history of black presence in America."

Indeed, this speaker presents her black father as the hero of her childhood. After all, it was her black father who risked his life for the sake of his children's education.

His whole attitude about, nobody is better than my children; they're the prettiest, they're the brightest, they're the best; I mean, this whole thing just kind of combined to make him take a position alongside other community leaders, and there were several other men who took the same position. And I say men at this point because it was the men that the Ku Klux Klanners were targeting, for the most part, in terms of violent repercussions.—All around people were dying. My father and my uncles and my brothers spent many a night guarding our homes. And my uncle's store was bombed, and several churches in the community were bombed.

And my father took the stand to stay that: "I'll participate in freedom meetings, I'll participate in Headstart." Headstart was a very controversial thing! "I will take the Headstart teacher, who is white, from New York City, I will put her in my car, and I will drive her to the Headstart school, and my wife, I will take her to the Headstart school, too, and my two little children, I'm taking them in my car, and we're gonna all go over to the Headstart school, and my wife is gonna be a teacher there, and the teacher from New York, I'll drop off there, I mean, I'm gonna do this." And he took those kinds of risks, not only with his own life, but with the lives of his children. The people he really cared about most in his life.

It was her black father who taught her about talking back:

My father was one for bragging. And some people may say that he was haughty, and he was arrogant, and he was egotistical, but, I think that in the environment that we grew up in, to be haughty and to be arrogant and to be egotistical was one of the biggest pluses that you could have, because that's about *all* you had. It's still there today, and some people think that I'm haughty and that I'm arrogant, and that I'm egotistical, but I see it as their problem.

Because my father brought me over, and, but at the same time he taught us to be loving, to be kind, to care, to be generous, you know, to reach out. To not lie, to not cheat, you know. And all those other things, and so far as I'm concerned, it was a very good upbringing.

And it was from her black father, and her black mother, that she learned the fundamental lesson of black family solidarity: "My father and mother really taught us that we needed each other, and that we should always be honest with each other, and should always care about each other, and should always be there for each other."

Far from unique, such attributions resonate throughout the narratives of other black women. In a parallel, if reversed, version, a more famous activist, Septima Poinsette Clark (in McFadden, 1980), similarly credits her parents:

My mother was very haughty.—She often said, "I never gave a white woman a drink of water."—It was good for those two to be together because my mother, with her haughtiness, and my father, with his gentleness, I felt that I stood on a platform that was built by both.—I stood on a platform built by my mother and father.

It is especially with reference to their education that these black teachers acknowledge their parents. The woman from Boston, for example, recalls:

It was for sure that I was going to college. I was always told, especially by my father, that the only way that black people had any chance of making it, you had to have a college education. I lived at home. There was, you know, absolutely, no way of living away at college. I mean, just no money. My mother had saved, ever since I was a baby, you know, U.S., good old U.S. Savings Bonds, to send me to school, which was a very conscious decision of saving, and going without themselves, in order to send me to school.

In these families, the need to become an educated woman is virtually identical with the imperative to become a teacher. The woman from Mississippi attributes both of these directives to her father. "I don't think my father ever stopped to think where he was gonna get the money, especially since he didn't have a penny, but it was always assumed that we were going to go to college. And because of that I guess, I was put to thinking that, yes, I will be a teacher." But her analysis also includes the influence of the larger black community, and the context of race relations in the South.

In the rural area that I was raised in, in that whole vicinity of the south, it was considered to be a really good profession to be a teacher. OK? And there were several reasons for that. One was that teaching was one of the few professions that was open to blacks. And they weren't really discriminated against if they went into the field, and the reason for that was that Mississippi ran a dual segregated school system, so only blacks could teach blacks, and so blacks who went to college and were trained to be teachers were virtually assured of jobs. And so therefore, the people in the community who were looked up to, quote un-quote, and who were considered to be community leaders, fit into several different categories, and one of the categories that they fit into was that of a teacher. The other was, of course, the leaders in the church. OK? Those two really stood out.

The woman who grew up in Louisiana reiterates this analysis, making gender distinctions, and adding, with her flashback scene, a sense of actually being "summoned" by the black community.

I remember we would sit on the front porch. People would pass by as they went on their little strolls in the evening. And all the neighbors would, you'd just kinda bow your head, and then they would say, "What do you wanna be when you grow up, little girl?" And early on, I'd say, "Well, if I were a man, I would be a minister." I had figured out that ministers had an interesting life. I liked that role. But, I said, "Since I'm not, I'll be a teacher."—And the image I was using was this lady who was later the principal of my school, who was very well-known, and she seemed to have the most power of any black woman I knew around.

In the reconstructed memory, the family sit in a slightly elevated position (indicative of the roles to which the child aspires), but they are engaged in active social dialogue with their neighbors. From the point of view of the child, the meaning of her life is everyone's concern.

In her discussion of opportunities foregone, this same woman articulates the "service" ethos within which her extended family judged individual talents and directed individual children. Typical of these life stories, this woman does not remember resenting the collective project which guided her life choices; rather, she explains how, as a child, it became a taken-for-granted part of her own black identity.

My godfather was a famous New Orleans jazz musician. . . . And he would not teach me to play by ear. I had to *read* music. Later I came to the conclusion that maybe he thought if I got really good young, I might go into the nightclub life. And it just seemed like they were preparing me for something else. I didn't care, whatever it was, I was a very obedient child, you know! I was aware that people were, in fact, at that time, in black life, they were looking for the children who were gifted in certain areas, and the teachers, principals, everybody would really put. . . . And you just almost *had* to do it, and it was fun for me, to do it, so there was no problem.

Another woman reiterates:

And so, I decided, I guess, at an early age, or it was decided for me, that I was going to college. I just never thought that it would be any other way. It was always assumed that we were going to college. And because of that, I guess, I was put on to thinking that, yes, I will be a teacher.

Adding an historical dimension, one woman comments on Martin Luther King, Jr., "he was a part of his times," and continues, "*all* of us who wanted to, as we called it, 'raise the race;' this was our whole life, you know. And we weren't just individuals; we were really part of that whole movement."

In these, as in many other life stories of black women, "the theme of family and family unity found in the female slave narrative is transformed and expanded into an ideal of service to others" (Braxton, p. 48).[35] In an interesting variation of this trend, one woman, whose father, mother and grandmother died when she was a teenager, states that she had "no idea" of becoming a teacher. After attending a black college in the South, becoming a secretary, and moving to New York City, she was persuaded to teach in her own neighborhood "as an example to black children." Reincorporated into the black educational lineage, she talks about her students as if they were her own children.

The concept of "fictive kinship, the dominant cultural system" in black communities (Fordham, 1988: 57), in highly salient in these stories. As I demonstrate in more detail below, it is precisely within such a symbolic matrix that each of these political activists has been constituted as an organic intellectual, *of* and *for* the people with whom she signifies. By becoming a black teacher-mother, each of these women is able "to seek self-realization through personal effort in service to the group" (LaVine and White in Fordham, p. 81), *and* to construct "an oppositional social identity" (Fordham, p. 55) with reference to the larger racist society.

I Answer With My Life

Into the Heart of Whiteness

The autobiographical reflections of these black women are everywhere organized as arguments *for* a sense of self as defined in black discourse and community, and *against* an alien identity as portrayed in dominant white discourse and institutions. We have seen the way in which childhood reminiscences are presented in terms of these semiotic struggles. Memories of racial challenges in college and early teaching jobs are delivered in considerably more agitated tones than are recollections of earlier or later episodes; they can be described as narrative ruptures.

The sense of personal efficacy declines in this phase of the stories; what increases is an apprehensive vulnerability. Although such problems have been somewhat anticipated in the adolescent anecdotes, it is not sufficient to explain these transitions in terms of "typical" (that is, white) difficulties in becoming an adult, or even in becoming a woman. A significantly different dynamic is also operating.

These young black women set off into the white world carrying expectations of mythic proportions; their odysseys, they believe, will take them "horizontally through space and vertically through society" (Gates, 1987: 82); university education and professional employment, they expect, will transform not only their lives but also those of other black people. But separated from their families, from their cultural communities, from their system of signification, from their existing black identities, these young women's passages turn out to be isolated, individual journeys "into the heart of whiteness" (Gates, 1984b: 297–298).

One woman's rendering of her transition crisis focuses on her separation from her father. In an intense vignette which cannot be fully understood without references to race, this narrator recreates her experience in primordial terms.

> It was my birthday. It was August thirteenth, and I got this letter saying that I had gotten twenty-six hundred and fifty dollars, in grants and scholarships, and all this, you know, to come to university. And my mama cried. Well, I didn't see Daddy cry, but I'm sure that he cried. I'm sure he was crying for a couple of different reasons. One was that I'd gotten this money to go to school, and, you know, nobody in our family had ever gone to a *big* university, and so that was a really big deal. And then also, you know, he knew he didn't have the money to send me to college, but he was just gonna do the best he could.

And so then I started to prepare to come to college, and . . .
I never will forget the morning I left, *everyone* piled into the
car to go except Daddy. Well, his excuse was, "there's not
enough room for me in the car." And so he sat on the front
porch, and as we pulled away, I watched him crying. You
know, he was just really heartbroken by then. I mean, it was
not just a child that was leaving, but it was a *girl* child that
was leaving, and it was the one he had . . .! Gosh, all those
miles and he wouldn't be there to protect me, and you know,
he was really going through a lot of trauma.

This student's own subsequent sense of trauma at college is expressed
in terms of fundamental interpretive dissonance: "The first semester
was really awful! I couldn't understand anything anybody was saying,
and nobody could understand me, either, I found out later." A second
woman's experience echoes this description; when she stood up in
front of the class, she recalls, "I would go, 'you know, I, uh, you
know,' " and although one professor helped her, she says "I still have
problems with language."

That this is not simply an issue of accent, but of language in its
most profound sense, is demonstrated by another anecdote. Within the
prevailing system of white signification, the first woman discovers, she
is subjected to the "abusive Western practice of deflation through
misnaming" (Gates, 1984b: 299); in her Sociology 101 class, she
"heard it analyzed about how poor and lower-classed I was. I went
home and cried." It is only when a friend evokes the power of black
constructions of meaning, in the persons of her parents, that she can
revise this insult.

I was talking to a friend who then put it in the perspective that
I just put it into, and what she said to me, in essence, was that
you never let anybody define you. Your father never did, and
mother never did, and your father and mother had it all figured
out. And, starting at that point, I always had it figured out,
that no Sociology 101 class professor who had his degree from
the university was ever going to tell me again, who I was and
what I was.

Racial restrictions on dating at college are the central cause of one
woman's discursive outburst, but her complaint includes several connected problems: she is separated from her family; she has lost access

to the (re)interpretive wisdom of black adults; her symbolic system has broken down.

> When I had gone north, I had naively thought that the people
> in the north weren't prejudiced. And, wow! Was I in for a
> shock! And the campus that I went to, my father had told me,
> that he thought if it was a sorority-fraternity campus. . . . He
> wanted me to go to a more liberal college. And I, for some rea-
> son, didn't take his advice and went to this place.
>   Wow! You know, it was really unbelievable. Blacks and
> whites couldn't date, and all this kind of stuff, you know.
> There were only like ten of us on the whole campus anyway.
> Ten blacks, and we used to laugh among ourselves. We were
> friends, but we were ten people that would never have chosen
> to be friends with each other, you know! So we didn't even
> have each other to date, 'cause we just didn't fit each other.

For these two women, entering college coincides with a move from a southern to a northern state; a third woman becomes a teacher after going north. For the fourth woman, shifting from the large northern city where she was educated to teach in a nearby small town effects the same sort of dislocation as the others experience. Given the ways in which the rest of the narratives draw strength from the slave narrative tradition, these versions of the underground railroad story read like grotesque parodies of the flight of the runaway slave.

It is with such a sense of bitter irony that one woman recalls her experiences *after* receiving a college degree, getting married, and find- ing employment. From her perspective, racism played a central role in producing the conditions she and her husband experienced; she was supporting him through college, but she was very poorly paid at the only job she could find, and they were discriminated against in housing. Her recollections of those early years evoke timeless memories of other young black women, separated from their families and communities, surviving on minimal resources, and living in decrepit quarters; if the listener loses track of whether the speaker is a captive African woman, or a runaway slave, or a "welfare mother," or a black college graduate, then the point is made.

> Up until that time I had lived all my life in one house. So this
> was my first time away from home. And it was a whole other
> interesting experience finding an apartment. The discrimination
> we went through was pretty traumatic. And, especially, as I

said, living that far away from home. Living that far away from black people. Living in a white, sort of semi-rural community.

Mine was the main salary for the first four years. It wasn't very main, that's for sure. We lacked little things like a telephone, you know, linoleum on the kitchen floor! We had no sink in the bathroom, and the toilet emptied out into the stream which ran behind, beside the house. Primitive, primitive living conditions. When I think back on it, you know, it's just incredible.

But at the time, we had no choice. We were discriminated against . . . to a *great* degree in apartments. Applying for ten-dollar-a-week apartments in really pretty crummy, tenement-style neighborhoods. We'd see people peeking out of the shade, and then never answering the door, when they saw black people there. We were sent by real estate agents, to boarding houses. I mean, rooming houses. In the worst slums, with, you know, indigent folks sort of hanging around the stairs. And, that's the kind of places, I guess, they figured that black people wanted to live.

The phrase which this woman uses to describe this town, "sorta like alien territory for both of us," carries wider implications, particularly since it reverberates with similar expressions used by other women, for instance, "I became especially close to foreign students." The recorded anguish of these young women is rooted in their developing realization that they will *always* be strangers in their own country; they will *never* really escape from racism; south or north, illiterate or educated, they will live out the rest of their days "in the master's house." Johnson's (1989: 42) definition of black discourse concretely depicts this relationship: "The word 'vernacular' does not name a separate realm: it comes from the Latin 'verna,' which means 'a slave born in his master's home.' The vernacular is a difference *within*, not a realm outside."

In the Master's House

In the prevailing white culture, where *to be employed* is *to be*, a young adult seeking a first job is likely to be beset by anxieties; but for these young black women, entering professional employment in that same white world poses very particular personal challenges. They arrive at this turning point knowing that within their lifetimes, college-educated black Americans have become sleeping car porters and domestic workers in order to earn a living. If they are not already aware, they soon come to understand that, in the master's house, it is powerful white men who ultimately determine what kind of work black women will do. Then, as these narratives relate, they can never be sure why they are or are not hired, for the racial criteria which they suspect will never be acknowledged. Considering how irrelevant their particular qualifications seem to be to the outcome of their employment searches, it is not surprising, therefore, to hear each of these teachers attribute her final success to *luck*.

"I was lucky," insists the woman who has always taught black children; although she has been a reading specialist for many years, she describes becoming a teacher as if it were a case of mistaken identity. When she decided to "go north," this woman recounts, "I came to my sister on Thursday night"; on Friday, she rested for a day; on Monday, she went to look for a job at the Board of Education. There, she announces, "I was *immediately* hired as a school secretary." Since she was already a college graduate, and had appropriate work experience, this may not seem very remarkable. Yet not here, nor anywhere else in our conversation, did this woman associate her job mobility with her own credentials or abilities.

In her version, she became a teacher because she somehow pleased those who were in power. When she worked in the central office, she "met the right people." "They liked me," she says, but she never explains why; "they told me 'this job is not good enough for you'; they were extra nice to me." More than a recognition of her own worth, this description seems to praise the generosity of her protectors. She was persuaded to teach, she recalls, when she was offered a job in her own neighborhood and told she should be an example to black children, an explanation which, again, does not accentuate her own assets.

Yet, judging from other parts of her narrative, there is a great deal of cleverness, and rebellion, hidden under this woman's cover story. Certainly, for a black woman to be offered a job teaching black children can be interpreted in several different ways. There is no doubt that this woman's teaching and political activism are passionately centered on black children. Yet, in plantation symbolism, the slave who is assigned to take care of black babies is of the very lowest status. So this woman, recognizing the contempt accorded her work, conceals her intelligence, but uses her position to help black children succeed, always undermining "the system," which she declares "is messed up."

136

"I guess I was lucky," reports one woman who was hired to work in day care; she was unable to find a job in a school, "and certainly that was because of discrimination, 'cause in those days, there were *plenty* of teaching jobs." "Well, I was unlucky in that the job paid very poorly," she adds; but

at that point, the director was looking to hire people with degrees. To upgrade the idea of the day care. To get it to be a school where kids were taught things. I don't think they cared *what* color I was. After all, if there were plenty of jobs in public schools . . . who was going to apply for a job at a day care center who had a degree? Well, a black person, who couldn't get another job. And so, it was like, "Sure, we'll take you." Anybody, you know, who had a good record in college. I got good recommendations. I had all As in practice teaching, and so, I was hired. And my take-home salary was fifty-five dollars a week.

Being hired to teach white children is problematic is every one of these stories, presumably because this work, unlike that of the mammy, requires their *intellectual* development. So it is important to note that this woman is recruited at a level where childcare is generally understood in *physical* and *emotional* terms, that is, the "proper" functions of a black woman. That she is so poorly paid is, of course, also a result of the general cultural disdain for small children and their female caretakers, as the day care director is well aware. This woman has since moved to the public school system, where she teaches kindergarten and first grade; one apparent benefit of working with young children is that she does not report hostile racial challenges in her classroom.

Another story repeats the experience of having high grades at college, and failing to find employment. Here the issue of a black woman teaching white children becomes explicit; the prospective students are at the high-school level. As is true throughout this woman's narrative, terrible ironies multiply around her ambiguous appearance.

I started looking for a job like everyone else. And I actually almost had no choice, because I wasn't getting (that was the story) I wasn't getting any jobs. I had the highest grades in student teaching, and I wasn't getting any jobs. And then, it turned out. . . .
People would come, and they would interview certain people,

that they watched student teaching, and so . . . I thought sure I'd get one. Well, it turned out, they would ask the professor, and he was a good friend of mine, the coordinator of student-teaching, "Is she Greek? Is she Italian? And he'd say, "No. She's black." And they would go, "Ooooh!" In that case, they couldn't hire me. So I lost out on five jobs. I didn't even realize.

Then, the very town that I was in, gets an opening! The very person in the field of music that I had been student-teaching with is moving. And so he says, "Well, I know you'll get the job." And it had been the very school. . . .

Nope! I didn't get the job! And so then three of my professors got really angry, and they went down to the board, and I don't know what all, and they said, "If another job comes up, she'll be the first to have it." Yeah.

Within the context of this story, the expressive power of that last small word is extraordinary. So total is this remembered cynicism that the listener, together with the young woman, experiences the subsequent turn of events as something akin to divine intervention.

Then I started becoming realistic about the fact that blacks . . . have to teach where there are blacks. When, one of the music teachers, she had been trying for years to get pregnant, got pregnant! Oh, boy. So then, it was, well, are they gonna hire . . . me? And that was a big hassle, but they actually investigated another town that had a black teacher teaching white kids, and they met with them.

They were so proud of themselves! I was the first black to be hired in the state of ——— (because it turned out in ———, there was a sizeable black population), I was the first black . . . quote (now, I didn't look it! but) I was the first black to be hired to teach in an all-white school. And ——— was the first town to do this. And they were really pleased with themselves.

The school board's subsequent actions separate her from her chosen constituency, and subject her to the scrutiny of elite white families.

The next thing was where were they gonna place me. And instead of placing me in this school, that was the minority school where I had student-taught and I knew all the kids, they placed me in the country club school, because they thought those parents would be better able to handle it. Now they didn't realize that I knew the Appalachian white parents. Actually, I used to go to Tupperware parties for these kids! They were actually less prejudiced than the wealthier, supposedly liberal ones.

I really was heartsick. I wanted to teach in that school. But they put me in the country club setting, and for my homeroom, I had the president's of ——— Insurance Company daughter. They were ninth graders. And I had the president of ——— Candy Company, all the big companies. National companies. All these kids seemed to be sitting in this room, you know! Looking at me.

So situated, she can be seen, at best, as one of a kind, the exception to the rule, a black woman who is not really "black." Perhaps not unexpectedly, this woman soon chooses to teach poor black children in a large urban district.

For another woman, luck appears as a "once-in-a-lifetime" opportunity. She does not dare to turn down a teaching position in a city where any opening is rare; nor is she permitted to postpone it because she is pregnant. Instead, like the mammy, she must set aside her own infant to attend to other people's children.

When I left (student teaching), I was pregnant with my first child, and I felt like I needed a rest. But I signed up to be a substitute teacher, and, of course, went to apply for a full-time job. About this time, the ——— public schools were looking for someone to teach black American history. They were putting on an all-out search, and I was there, and I applied. They were looking for someone, they said, with more experience, and I was convinced that I could do the job.

And I remember . . . prior to their offering me a contract, the person who was doing the hiring, in employee services, called me and said, "Well, now, I understand that you're about to have a baby, and we will give you this contract, and . . .! We, um, are you, do you think you're going to be able to report to work?" and I said, "*Of course* I am." Of course I lied a bit. I didn't know if I was gonna be able to report to work in August. Sure enough, the baby did come in July, and I *did* report to work in August when he was three weeks old, and that was a real nightmare!

I Answer With My Life

She was correct in judging the exceptionality of this chance; to date, hers is "the first and last black American history class" offered in the local school system.

In her other courses, outside, as it were, her racially-defined, "proper" province, this teacher has been attacked by some white students and parents. Needless to say, such expressions of insolence preclude the supposed sentimental attachment between the mammy and her charge. Documenting this regularly repressed dimension of race relations in American schools, it is important to note, the narrator assesses her experience in *political* rather than in *racial* terms.

Generally from the students, especially during my first years there, you did not get a lot of overt racism. Of any sort. Except during my last three or four years there. I think that people were in general not feeling that it was good to be anti-racist. OK? And people were feeling a little bit more at ease about their racism.

And that's not to say that the first years that I taught there that racism did not exist, and that people were not racist. But they kept their mouths shut. And they were on their guard, about not letting it come forth, because that was in the early seventies, and it just didn't look like the anti-racist whites and people of color were going to be very tolerant of overt racism.

But then in the late seventies and early eighties, people began to feel free to come forth with it, and during my last couple of years at ——— High School, once I got a note pushed under my door, saying, nigger something, and once a boy in my class was passing around this note. I was showing a movie, something about Japanese dancing, it was in one of my ethnic culture classes. He passed this note along, talking about those slanted eyes and using cuss words, and talking about how the H-bombs . . . didn't do what they were supposed to do to them, and I was *furious*. And I had to deal with that, you know.

And so the whole turnabout in terms of moving towards being conservative in the country was impacting on me in the classroom. It didn't change what I was doing. But it did make it psychologically a little bit more difficult to continue, in my same, creative, and definitely left-of-center approach. But they did not override, overshadow my experience there. I mean, they were isolated incidents at best. And I always prided myself in being able to handle my discipline problems.

140

Carnival Time[36]

These narrators are unmistakably committed to realism; they acknowledge "what is," however distressing that may be. Describing their college days, they openly announce their inability to overcome more powerful forces; discussing their early teaching years, they use such words as "realistic," "real," and "really," albeit inflected with chagrin. But white *illusions* ("what seems to be") are not black *realities* ("what really is"), these authors also insist; "the world as the master would have it" is not the same as "the world as the slave knows it really is" (Gates, 1987: 93).

To be *in* the master's house is not necessarily to be *under* the master's control; for the master's rule is not "unified, complete, fixed and forever" (Clark and Holquist, 1984: 301), but is full of "loopholes" which can be exploited by those held in bondage. Besides documenting the discrimination which they have suffered, these women's accounts disclose deep discrepancies in prevailing educational arrangements. That they do succeed (they graduate from college; they are eventually hired as teachers) must be understood, at least in part, by the inability of educational institutions to deal with anomalies.

Finally, however accidental, arbitrary, or subordinate their initial incorporation, as experienced teachers, these women prove themselves well able to exploit the ambiguities and weaknesses of the white-dominated system. Under specific historical conditions, they are even able to reconstitute social relations in the schools where they work. During the breakdown of ordinary racial arrangements in the sixties and seventies, these authors actively appropriate the interpretive gaps which open up around them, using the "respite from the relatively closed and rigid historical patterns that dominant ideologies impose" (Clark and Holquist, p. 302) to repair racist ruptures in their own and in others' lives.

In these segments of the life histories, narrators delight in the dissolution of normal social order, mock the impotence of those usually in power, and revel in the freedom of expression possible for those who are ordinarily suppressed. In the form of their telling, and in the meaning of their content, these stories are tales of semiotic *carnival*. Indeed, one narrator presents her adult adventures in an urban riot in the same tones of exhilaration which she uses to describe her childhood experience of Mardi Gras.

In the earlier example, she is a black bus passenger who enjoys the suspension of negative racial categorization; in the later, complementary description, she is a black school teacher who celebrates positive racial identification. In neither case does the speaker portray herself as an original instigator of social disorder. But she is not just an onlooker, for "carnival is not a spectacle seen by the people; they live in it, and everyone participates. . . . " (Bakhtin in Clark and Holquist, p. 300). As a child, she *signifies:* recognizing, deconstructing, and reinterpreting social signs; as an adult, she assumes the role of an *organic intellectual.*

As a black teacher, this woman holds herself particularly responsible for the ways which black children *interpret* what is happening around them. Before the emergency she describes, the narrator, together with other teachers at her junior school, had already begun to develop "new strategies for reading the world" (Clark and Holquist, p. 297): "At one point we had a really glorious two years, where we were doing the black consciousness thing and there were an extraordinary number of militant black teachers at my school. And we would plan strategies."

For these black teachers, working in an inner city in 1968, the interpretive imperative must have been intense. As the adjective "militant" indicates, this was an extraordinarily assertive phrase in black American discourse. Confrontation and repudiation, "talking back," was the mode of the moment. Thousands of black Americans participated, in their various ways, in this defiance. They met with violent opposition on every side. The assassination of Martin Luther King, Jr. is, in fact, at the center of this memory: "When Dr. King died, that was quite a time. Our area, and that's how that school got to be called King, was the only one that didn't burn. And we attributed that to what we did. We sat and planned strategies."

King's death is not just a detail in this woman's story; elsewhere in her narrative, she tells how she would have become a minister had she been male; she talks about the religious basis of her political beliefs; she places herself in the same activist generation. She too dares to co-author and coordinate black interpretive community; she challenges those who already script, and benefit from, white institutional order; she risks retaliation.

In the moment of crisis, the white principal of this narrator's school, feeling threatened by the black teachers' initiative, tries to intimidate them.

> He had a livid fit! He didn't wanna do *anything*. He didn't
> want to have any kind of program. He really told us that our
> jobs were on the line, if we *did* this thing which we were deter-
> mined to do. So we said, OK. We'll risk our jobs, on how the
> kids respond to this thing that we definitely think we ought to
> do.

The struggle pivots on a point of interpretation:

> Where we lost him was we were gonna sing "We shall over-
> come." And he thought that was a sign to the children, you
> know, "we're gonna overcome." And he thought if *any* song is
> not sung, that was the one that shouldn't be sung.

In symbolic terms, the principal's capitulation signals the onset of
carnival, for the ordinary school hierarchy is overturned when he quite
literally descends from the highest to the lowest position: "He went
down to the basement and locked himself in a room and painted
garbage cans." And, while "power, repression and authority never
speak the language of laughter" (Bakhtin in Clark and Holquist, p.
308), their downfall does:

> It was the funniest thing! Wow! You know, he was compulsive.
> He had to do something, so he painted garbage cans for the
> various floors, but meanwhile, he didn't have *anything* to do
> with it, and we took it over, and we decided to have a big as-
> sembly, where all kids were in there.

Before an assembly can be scheduled, however, this woman has to cope
with an unfamiliar and "absolutely notorious class," who "were really
in riot form." Their homeroom teacher is unable to control them, and
the narrator, a music teacher, has a reputation of being able to "soothe"
difficult children. But simple improvisation becomes complex explication when her racial identity is misinterpreted.

In these narratives, black constructions of reality regularly contradict
white versions, but different black interpretations do not compete
against each other. In this case, rioting is not presented as alternative
meaning-making, but as senseless anarchy. Carnival is *not* chaos; it is
an act of communal *signifying*, which like any dramatic ritual, must
be composed, coordinated and performed. In this story, black teachers
assume responsibility for these tasks; skillful semioticians by reason of
their experience and education, they assist those who, because of age
and circumstance, are less facile in racial reinterpretation.

"As it turned out," this speaker recalls, "the kids didn't realize that
I was black. They didn't even realize who I was." She is, in fact,
physically attacked by one child.

> I started to say something about Dr. King, and he said, he abso-
> lutely did *not* wanna hear what anybody white had to say

> about it. And before I could say, "Uh," he had me by the
> throat. He had actually put his little hands. . . . He was a small
> child. I said, "Wait a *minute, little boy!*" I picked him up,
> some kind of way, and the class was, they were really rioting,
> and the big kids on top of the desks, you know, and they were
> gonna . . . see a fun thing that time. So I said, "Well, wait." I
> told him he was making a big error.

Within the context of carnival, this teacher's role is not so much to
explain her ambiguous appearance as it is to initiate these children into
the complicated world of racial masquerade. So, she does not merely
reveal a "true" self hidden under a "deceptive" mask; more importantly, she discloses the fundamental immorality of the *gaze:* "I explained to him that I wasn't white, and even if I was, he shouldn't have
done that." Her interpretation does not simply reverse the hierarchical
order; it actually interrogates "the philosophical assumptions on which
that order was based (Ashcroft, Griffiths, and Tiffin, 1989: 33); it
ultimately seeks to "destroy the symbolic code that created the false
oppositions themselves" (Gates, 1987: 93).

"Then they wanted to know," she continues, "well, how was that?
How could I be black?" Telling them the story of her life, she presents
her own (and their) identity, not in terms of "fixed, clearly definable
qualities," but as a "process, a continual creation"; she affirms, in
Byerman's (1985: 5) phrase, "the disorderly, vital history" which is
black experience: "So I said, 'Well, if you sit down, and calm down,
I'll explain that little story to you too.' I told them the whole story of
that! And then we got into slavery."

> When it was time for the bell, the principal came around to see
> what was going on. And there was dead silence, and I was ex-
> plaining away. So he said, "Uh, do you wanna change?" I said,
> "Please, don't change now," because I hadn't even gotten to
> the music part yet.

Speaking about her ordinary music classes, this teacher says, "it used
to be fun to sell (students) on Mozart and Bach. Kind of like Jonathan
Kozol did with Shakespeare" (Kozol, 1967). But talking about a time
when the school was surrounded by angry demonstrators, she tells
how she sang spirituals with frightened children. And music from a
black repertoire is featured at the emergency assembly.

144

We sang all the songs, you know, of the movement. And we sang "Precious Lord"; one of the older teachers who had a great voice sang Dr. King's favorite song. And then I did, "Once to every land and nation," that was one of his favorite songs. Even though it was classical. I whipped up my fast class, got the harmonies, and we got that song going.

Another teacher encourages the children to grieve, summoning them into the black interpretive community with a traditional African call-and-response:

He explained that he was very angry, and, yes, he was angry at white people. He went through his whole thing. And then he cried and he had an absolute fit, but we had actually planned some of that. We thought if we would go through the fit ourselves, we would take it off of them. And the kids cried.

And after he would get them to a certain level, he would call them back. Now we gonna bring you down. Now we gonna bring you up again! You know, you would bring 'em up and then you'd bring 'em down. And then we brought 'em down to where we wanted 'em.

Yet the purpose of this performance, as Clark and Holquist (p. 313) argue in defense of carnival, is *not* "to let off steam in a harmless, temporary event." These children become calm because they are engaged in a compelling interpretive lesson.

Because carnival allows a pedagogy of (re)interpretation to be practiced within the school, the disruption of the normal curriculum is not "time wasted." Quite the reverse, it is a "time filled with profound and rich experience" (Clark and Holquist, p. 302); it is an extraordinary event which has lasting ideological and material effects, not only for the children, but for the whole neighborhood.

The kids were so impressed. They went home and told their parents, and they sat down, and all the new things they had learned that day, and the whole area was quiet. It was the only area, and they really said that they thought that what happened in the schools affected what happened with the families. We were pretty pleased.

Finally, her participation in this communal ritual has lasting consequences for the storyteller herself; in the narrative reconstruction of her personal memory, she is able to transform this traumatic event into a triumph of signification.

The Outraged Mother

"I kind of enjoyed it too," admits another woman, talking about a different episode in the same turbulent period. During an intensely acrimonious, racially polarized teachers' strike, she did not obey (white)[37] administrative directions; nor did she act according to (white) teachers' union mandates. Instead, in the name of the (black) children she taught, she seized control of the building where she worked. This is "the most daring thing" she has ever done, but she was determined to keep the school operating "whatever it took." Even though she received bomb threats, "nothing would stop me," she insists. Yet she was under such stress that she "had bags under (her) eyes all the time."

Only two other teachers ever came to work, and she "ended up running the school" throughout the strike. (Afterwards, she reports, the principal "put a dirty letter" in her file.) She called meetings for parents, and explained the situation to them. At first, "the custodian was very good" to her; "he made sure that no troublemakers got inside" the school. Later on, however, "he got in trouble with his supervisor" for helping her. So, she would arrive before him in the morning, and open the building herself.

Such a simple summary, reconstructed from my written notes, belies the complexity of this narrative act. In ordinary times, still employed at the same school, this storyteller does not dare to flaunt her carnival activities. So she tells a modest life history; only her mischievous smile indicates that this is an ironic fairy tale: with the help of (white) benefactors, the humble (black) heroine becomes a school secretary, then a teacher; in times of (racial) trouble, she shows her true worth (!) by performing, single-handed, the work of an entire school staff.

Her grown son is less reticent; it was because he proudly boasted about his mother's political activism that I was able to locate this woman in the first place. Another mother, visiting *her* son, heard this story, and wrote to me about it:

His mother was active in school during the teachers' strike. The (Jewish) principal of the school called all *black* women (teachers and volunteers and aides) "mother." She took exception to it, and told him she was not his mother, etcetera. The others

took up the refrain, and it ended up with them all standing outside, shouting, "Mother! Mother!" The newspapers took up
the idea; they thought they meant "motherf____"!

This is the only version of the incident which I have, but even in
this abbreviated, third-hand rendition, the black narrative tradition is
evident: the storyteller tells a joke which depends on the "rhetorical
play" of multiple meanings; he uses "rhetorical indirection" to attack
the white master; and he "scream(s) on" the man who insults his
mother: "Yo' mama" (Gates, 1988: 65, 69). Who has the right to
name the mother, this anecdote asks, and what significance does that
name carry? Demanding public recognition as her true son, this young
black man establishes his personal and political genealogy by signifying
on the white stereotype of the good black mother, the mammy.

Of course, *being called* a mammy is not the same as *being* a mammy,
and black women have generated their own complex set of responses
to this naming. Although the relationship between the black woman
held in bondage and her white master is essentially antagonistic, sometimes she may seem to acquiesce to his control. Talking about her
ordinary work days, this teacher explains: "I always make the best of
it. I always cope. I don't complain. For that day, I enjoy." But then she
adds: "I work like a dog. I work like two people. During my lunch
hour. I have no free time." *For whom* does she work so hard? In normal
times, judging from the rest of her narrative, this teacher uses her
assigned role as a disguise; she pretends to be a faithful mammy so
that she can "protect her own children" (Christian, p. 5). It is only at
times of danger and disorder, and in her narrative reconstruction of
those moments, that this woman allows glimpses of the self "implied
in all her actions and fueling her heroic ones" (Braxton, p. 2). Revised
and reversed, the mammy becomes the "outraged mother" in Afra-
American autobiography (Braxton, p. 1–2).

Although rarely revealed in the white public space, "an anger handed
down through generations of mothers who could have no control over
their children's lives" (Hirsch, p. 197) organizes not just the personal,
but also the work, social, and political relations of the black women
teachers presented here. In these narratives, anger is not a "privatized"
emotion; it is "collective" and "active" (Hirsch, p. 193); it is righteous,
and it is constructive, more often attending to those *for* whom the
speaker feels fearful than attacking those *against* whom she feels rage.

Within this symbolic matrix, each of these authors creates her own
coming into being as an adult black woman; she conceives (of) herself
in relationship not only to her "own" children, but also to the black

147

children she teaches, and to all black children. As a black mother-teacher-intellectual, she (re)produces for all her people, but especially for the young, the significance of their lives in captivity. "We feed the children with our culture," writes Nikki Giovanni (1975), "that they might understand our travail"; "we urge the children on the tracks/ that our race will not fall short."

Understood within such a matrix, many of these women's apparently generic comments resonate with additional, racial, meaning. It is the black woman teacher as slave mother, echoing and encoding an enduring protest, "why should my son be held in slavery?" (Braxton, p. 41), who complains about her job:

I wouldn't encourage my child. I wouldn't do it again myself.
There are so many negative things. The harder you work, the
less you are appreciated, by some people. I don't tell people I
am a teacher. Maybe society has something to do with it. And
too much politics. I don't dislike the kids, even the worst ones.
I dislike the system.

But her students thank her for what she has done: they send her cards on her birthday; they give her presents; they write her letters when they graduate from high school or college, or when they are in the service. "They love your very soul," she announces in one extraordinary phrase. So she continues to teach, for "it is a distinctive feature of the outraged mother that she sacrifices opportunities to escape without her children" (Braxton, p. 33).

Although they do not always use racially specific language, other narrators clearly deplore the ways in which those who enact the policies of powerful white institutions continually thwart the child-rearing agenda of the outraged mother. One woman's assessment of the causes of school failure is informed not only by her own success as a teacher, and her problems as the adoptive mother of two children diagnosed "learning-disabled," but perhaps most especially, by her experiences as an adult literacy volunteer in a prison. Here her students were, typically of the American penal system, black men. Interestingly, although they are adults, her interpretation of their needs is distinctly maternal:

There is not one reason why people go to prison. These guys
have basic serious problems. It's not just that they did a purse
snatching or an armed robbery. You know, these guys have
real learning problems. And what these guys needed was, you

know, they needed mothers. They needed warm, tender, loving care, which, of course, was impossible to give them. They were so needy. They needed so many things.

While she concludes that she cannot practice proper nurture under such conditions of total captivity, she does not reject its efficacy; instead, she shifts responsibility for these men's inadequate education. Contradicting those who would blame black families, she asserts: "I think that every parent cares, to some degree, in some way, although maybe they can't express it, for whatever reasons"; indicting instead those who do not exercise the ethos of the outraged mother, she argues:

> I put a lot of blame on the public school systems they went to. If every teacher really put *everything* that they had into doing *whatever they possibly could* for this child. . . . To be able to deal with some of the problems that kids have and really support kids and support families. . . . (emphasis added)

"I am not very forgiving of teachers who do not address the needs of all their students," echoes another teacher, making particular reference to her "very needy" black students.

In two of these narratives, the army is an institution within which, contrary to the curriculum of the outraged mother, young black men are taught to destroy themselves and others. When he came back from the service, one teacher reports about a former pupil, "he told about kids, little babies that were booby-trapped with bombs, and he had a real callous attitude towards the Vietnamese; this was the way that he could kill people legitimately." "I followed those kids up 'til they were twenty-five; we got really close," she remembers as she mourns,

> he'd been the one who loved Beethoven. The other kids couldn't stand Beethoven and he had sold everybody on Beethoven, and he had joined the Columbia record club for the classical stuff, and then that poor child went to Vietnam. He was the most sensitive of them all. And he cracked up over there. I don't think that he could stand . . . what he saw, and he flipped out.

It is not surprising, then, to hear this woman report anti-war activities elsewhere in her narrative. In one school where she taught, she says, "you had a homeroom, and you had to be a counsellor. And so I had to teach things like careers in the military, and so I taught conscientious objection, and had riots in my homeroom!" Another woman, whose father carried a gun to defend his family during the dangerous days of the Civil Rights Movement, has no trouble distinguishing between being militant in the black "revolutionary cause," and fighting for the white-controlled military. At her school, she recalls,

> all the recruiters were always in the building. They had litera-ture, you know, like set up in the halls, and I would always go through in the morning, and get me a big armful of it, and put it in the trash can! Stuff like that, I mean, you know, became fairly routine.

This same woman uses an explicitly maternal metaphor to talk about the courses in Women's Studies and African-American Studies which she started at her high school, and had to leave when she was trans-ferred. In a remarkable reversal of the reification of people which occurs so frequent in educational jargon, this teacher anthropomorphizes the subject matter which has so much personal meaning for her: "I hated to leave because I had designed and taught those two classes there, and they were my babies. And it was kind of like, you know, a mother leaving a baby. I wanted to nurture them." Viewed from the perspective of the outraged mother, it is not surprising that the same white adminis-trative officials whose job requirements separated her from her infant son subsequently remove her from the care of black students whose particular needs she fulfilled.

In content and in form, this woman teaches the tradition of militant nurture (Casey, 1990b) which was her parents' legacy to their children. One of the ways in which this teacher protects her black students from the white master is through a sensitive and benevolent assertion of her own authority over them. In the following passage, the most important word is "we"; by using the plural pronoun, this woman summons up the power of the whole African-American community to call its chil-dren home:

> There were times when I said, "if you skip my class, I'm com-ing down to the mall to get you. So sometimes, I would go down to the mall, and it would be a big scene because the class would be waiting there, anticipating my coming back with these six-feet, you know, men. And I would get down to the mall, and I would say, "Hi, John!" "Uh, *Hi!*" You know. They were always really surprised. I said, "Well, we come to get you." And they looked, "*We?*"

Those kind of confrontations could really get to be sticky, because you had to measure how you were going to approach that, and you had to know who you were talking to and what kind of child this was, and how they were gonna react to you. The students, of course, thought I was just walking into it, and not thinking each step of the way as to how I was going to do it, because some of these students were very, very belligerent about coming to class, and some of the classes they didn't go to. And it was just kind of, they'd like pass the word, "Don't skip ———— 's class, I mean, she'll come and get you," and that's embarrassing you know.

The plural pronoun appears again when the errant students return to the school with the teacher. Once the sense of a common project has been restored, this kind of authority has no need for punative retaliation.

We would start up the stairs together, and then I would notice, that they were walking *ahead* of me. And that was my signal, to not go in the door at the same time with them, because that would be really embarrassing, and the objective was *not* to embarrass somebody once you get them to class.

"In the classroom, loving the children to understanding" (Angelou, 1990: 36), these women (re)interpret ways of being black in a white world; with their own children, they practice a parallel revisionist pedagogy. The most important purpose of the black family curriculum, according to the emphases of these narrators, is creating the next generation of activists. The same woman whose son boasted about her courage proudly remembers bringing that child and his brother to political events: "In the sixties, we went everywhere together, when they were teenagers." During that period, one woman went "to *all* the marches" and took her infant daughter, and her mother, along: "all three generations would be in the march." More recently, another mother talks at length about taking her sons all over the country to teachers' union conventions. "You can make politics interesting," she says; "you can make it a family activity."

When her two sons wanted to play Dungeons and Dragons instead of going to an anti-apartheid march, this woman "set them down to the table," and read them a newspaper article written by another black mother who was "perplexed and appalled" because her daughter "took so much for granted." "At one point, my seven-year-old said, 'Momma, did you write that?' " she reports; "when I finished, of course the twelve-year-old really understood it. He says, 'Well, you got me now. I guess I have to go!' "

No simple account, this author's skilled narration of the event itself draws her sons into the circle of signifying which unites millions of African children held in bondage. In this story, her separation from her boys repeats and revises the statutes of slavery; that, as Sweet Honey in the Rock (1981) sings, "your children are not your children" becomes, in her version, an affirmation of their independent membership in the larger political collectivity. And the final reunion of mother and children on the political platform reverses the tragic tradition of the divided slave family; the ruptures of racism are repaired through collective (re)interpretation.

> I was trying to make sure that I kept my eyes on them. I didn't want them to get lost in this big crowd of people, and I lost them completely. I knew a lot of people who were there, and I said, "Have you seen my boys?" and one lady said, "Well, in fact, I saw both of them about ten minutes ago, and they were way up *ahead* of the march." And I went, "What are they doing down there?" Well, when I got down to the capitol rotunda, I found out.
>
> There they were, standing up front, with a big banner. *Long* banner, you know, it had something . . . "Get out of South Africa," "Down with Apartheid." And they were just grinning. When I got up to give my speech, my first boy knew that I was gonna say something about it. So I introduced them as my sons, and they really got off on it, and they loved it. That night they were running to watch TV because they wanted to see themselves on it.

Teachers Working for Social Change

"We weren't just individuals; we were really part of that whole movement." Spoken by one woman, these words epitomize the educational agenda of each of these teachers. Enlisted by their elders, and motivated by their own oppressive experiences, for these women, being a black teacher means "raising the race"; accepting personal responsibility for the well-being of one's people, and, especially, for the education of all black children.

When they were children, these women drew strength from the black community; now, as adults, they initiate others into the same living tradition. In classrooms, in neighborhoods, at home, in unions, in prisons, in the Urban League, in local electoral politics, they (re)construct communal meaning *of* and *for* a people held in captivity.

Working in places where white racist priorities prevail, these teachers practice a complex (re)interpretive pedagogy. Sharing the "signifying" repertoire which they have received and recreated, these women author *identity* and *community* for themselves, for their black students, and for the larger black constituency. Yet because it does not reproduce, but rather, radically subverts racist categorizations, this version of African-American discourse does not preclude political alliances with progressive white readers.

6

Conclusion

Because it focuses on history, some readers of this book might be tempted to relegate its significance to the "irrelevant" past. In conclusion, therefore, it remains to consider how these teachers' narratives, stretching back more than fifty years through the history of American education, can contribute to our understanding of the immediate present and the unfolding future of social change in this country.

Pessimism of the Intellect; Optimism of the Will

In the week following the Thomas confirmation, my friend, Klemesu, a taxi driver and an immigrant from Ghana, remarks: "There is only one party in this country now—Republican." During the same month, I hear the German liberation theologian, Dorothee Soelle (1991), assess the changes in Eastern Europe: "There is only one economic system in the world now—capitalism." Talking about the war in the Gulf, the coup in Haiti, the popularity of David Duke, the deaths of twenty-five workers in a local chicken-processing factory, my progressive friends are distressed and depressed.

In a time of conservative triumphalism, we ask each other, how can we conceive of social change? Has the conservative agenda prevailed? Do conservative priorities determine the kinds of questions which can be asked, and the kinds of answers which can be offered, in thinking about American education?

Concluding her analysis, Soelle evokes Gramsci's (1980: 175) words: "Pessimism of the intelligence; optimism of the will." In this chapter, I discuss why I persist in particular versions of Marxist, feminist, and anti-racist theory and practice; I argue that "elements taken from different existing problematics may, in a new order, and constituting a new field, yield us greater explanatory power and political purchase" (Johnson, 1980: 202), and I conclude that the examples of political action in this book offer realistic hopes for an ongoing progressive struggle.

Revising the Progressive Problematic

Although they speak as though they had a monopoly on the past, not only conservatives have a heritage. Just as the discourse of the right extends backwards in time, so, in dialogic relationship, does that of its interpretive adversary, the left. Alas, the relationship of the left to its own tradition(s)[38] is not an easy one, and there are good reasons why this should be so. But there are sources of strength, as well as examples of weakness, to be found in these memories, and it is to destroy the former that its antagonists exploit the latter. They have been very successful. Scholars indebted to the work of Karl Marx (including myself), for example, give pause before pronouncing his name in public; it feels strange to be regarded as absurd and obscene at the same time. Yet crises of the left, assaults from the right, and disastrous defeats are not new; others have fought similar battles under worse circumstances, and it should be as inconceivable to forget them as it would be to forsake those for whom we now struggle.

Consider Gramsci, exemplifying and articulating the strength of this tradition, expressing what it means to live within an historical network of human relationships, writing in a prison cell in 1933:

> We feel ourselves linked to men who are now extremely old, and who represent for us the *past* which still lives among us, which we need to know and to settle our accounts with, which is one of the elements of the *present* and one of the premises of the *future*. We also feel ourselves linked to our children, to the generations which are being born and growing up, and for which we are responsible (Gramsci, p. 147).

156

As this quotation demonstrates, my recollection of Gramsci, and Gramsci's own construction of continuity, define tradition in ways which are distinctly different from elite celebrations of high culture: our tradition is not focused on the accumulation and preservation of cultural capital; it is not concerned with the commodified products of dead artists; living people, not property, stand at its center.

For Gramsci, tradition is not a "cult" (p. 147), nor is it "utopian" (p. 175). The importance of the past can only be understood in relationship to the responsibilities of the present. Gramsci (p. 175) asserts: "it is necessary to direct one's attention violently towards the present as it is, if one wishes to transform it," and in the next sentence, declares, "Pessimism of the intellect; optimism of the will," not an inappropriate slogan for our own times. It is not surprising, therefore, that so many contemporary progressive intellectuals[39] have turned to Gramsci; he always admits that there are more than enough catastrophes to deplete our hopes; he always insists that more than adequate resources remain, that our collective wisdom is rich, complex, and vital, that we can be faithful to earlier insights, and flexible in present perplexities.

For these reasons, as well as for the actual content of his offering, it should be clear that my invocation of Gramsci is the very opposite of idolatry of the individual; it is to honor his participation in the progressive political project. It is in this sense that I regularly punctuate my summary of the life histories of women teachers working for social change with references to his work.

The Importance of the Political

The limitations of deterministic *economic* analyses of education and reproductive *cultural* studies of schooling are evident. Even so, for many readers it must seem ironic that I choose to celebrate the *political* in a time of conservative hegemony. But central to my project are two generative notions: (1) that we do not fully understand what it means to be *political;* in spite of the addition of such concepts as "resistance" and "empowerment," the significance of the political continues to be inadequately documented and insufficiently theorized in progressive academic research; (2) that the narratives of women teachers working for social change offer new ways of being political in the world; moving beyond the simply dispirited and merely reactive, these authors actively respond to current conditions, and, simultaneously, revise the progressive problematic.

Theoretically and strategically, the definition of the *political* has been, and continues to be, a continuous subject of struggle *within* the progressive tradition. What constitutes the political? What are its boundaries? What is the relationship of the political to the economic? What is the relationship of the political to the cultural? Towards which of these spheres should attention and energy be focused? How should political action be organized? What is the relationship between moments of mass mobilization and periods of apparent quiescence? And so forth.

Responses to these questions are not constructed in an abstract or arbitrary way, but always in relation to the concrete contexts within which they are posed; they are also formulated with reference to earlier understandings of similar predicaments. In Gramsci's version of the political, the development of critical understanding requires ingenuity *and* integrity, creativity *and* conviction; the (re)construction of Catholic, Marxist and African-American discourses in the featured narratives of contemporary women teachers epitomizes this very capacity.

By linking Gramsci and the teachers in this book, I predicate some parallels in their unorthodox approaches to the problems of their times. Like Gramsci, the activists featured in this study do not wait "for the historical process to provide the circumstances in which the ruling class would topple, the true revolutionaries would be acknowledged by the masses and socialism could be ushered in"; they engage in "active intervention(s) in history" (Hoare and Smith in Gramsci, p. lx). Unwilling to accept political labels, these women nevertheless work for social change; they teach their students how to speak English, and politics; they publicly profess their support for gay Catholics; they teach children ways of being black in the white world; they establish alternative schools in inner cities and in prisons; they bear witness on the Nicaraguan border; they tell the stories of their own lives.

Remembering the protean ways in which Gramsci conceptualizes the political allows us to recognize the contribution these activist teachers have made to the necessary renewal of the progressive problematic. In these life histories not only the *state* and its *institutions* are terrains of political struggle; so is *language*. Even *personal identity* is an arena of political activity. As in a number of other current understandings, in these inclusive versions, "everything is political" (Gramsci, p. 357).

Although the political is everywhere, it is not diffuse, for everyone is involved, but *not in the same way*. The lives of the women featured in this study are grounded in particular social relationships, and their transformative activities (including their narrative renderings) are organized around these specific connections. It is within concrete social contexts that each of these women simultaneously develops her sense of self, her understanding of others, and her response to existing social arrangements.

The Politics of Personal Identity

In each of these life histories, the ways that the narrator feels, thinks and acts as an adult is associated with the way she grows up, not simply as a "child," but as a female child, as a Catholic, or a Jewish, or a black child, as a middle-class, or a poor child. And, the social identities of the students she teaches have enormous consequences on each woman's perception of her self. Not only do these stories reveal how it feels to work with students who draw swastikas on your books, or who push a note under your door which says "nigger," with young people who are gay, or who are hungry, with "children who are viewed as having little value in America" (Kozol, 1991: 115); they also make us wonder why these critical dimensions have been washed out of most educational research.

"Ideology," argues Althusser (1972: 174), " 'recruits' subjects among the individuals (it recruits them all), or 'transforms' the individuals into subjects (it transforms them all)." But it does *not* recruit or transform them all *in the same way.* Any notion of an ordinary student, a typical teacher, or a generic activist, is definitively dislodged by the distinctive contrasts among these groups of narratives, and by the differences between these women's experiences, interpretations, and practices, and those of children, educators, or militants in other social circumstances.

In "that very precise operation" which Althusser calls *interpellation,* the person hailing " 'Hey, you there!' " is not always, or even often (as in his example), a policeman. In these narratives, prison inmates recruit a visiting nun; George Jackson transforms teachers of black children, so does Martin Luther King, Jr.; street people summon one woman, refugees another. By actively answering one (but not all) of these specific calls, each woman develops her own particular political identity.

Nor is the "turning around," (as Althusser suggests,) automatic. After reading *Rachel and Her Children* (Kozol, 1988), for example, many of the teachers in my graduate class recall experiencing agonizing ambivalence towards the homeless when they visited large cities; some persist in their antagonism towards the poor; and others explain local social projects in which they are already engaged. A willingness to listen to the voices of the dispossessed is not "natural"; a "capacity for empathy," an "ethic of caring" and "of personal accountability" (Collins, 1989) are created and sustained in certain social collectivities, and not others. As we have seen elsewhere, each of the teachers in this book situates herself within a specific historical network of human relationships, and takes her decisions with reference to that particular (Catholic, or Marxist, or African-American) living tradition. And all of these women participate in a feminist ethos of "care and connectedness" (Gilligan, 1982).

"One must conceive of" a human being, writes Gramsci, "as a series of active relationships in which individuality, though perhaps the most important, is not, however, the only element to be taken into account" (p. 352). To credit each of these women with deliberately choosing to engage in certain social relationships is to distinguish individuality from isolation, alienation, and "individualism," which is, in Gramsci's (p. 147) words, "merely brutish apoliticism." Refusing to respond to others, it is the individualist who fails to develop her self, finally and ironically becoming a conformist, for her "conception of the world is not critical and coherent but disjointed and episodic" (Gramsci, p. 324).

In Gramsci's thought, the political "figures, philosophically, as the central human activity, the means by which the single consciousness is brought into contact with the social and natural world in all its forms" (Hoare and Smith in Gramsci, p. xxiii). Through political practice thus broadly defined, these women become more fully human: they come into being as coherent selves at the same time as they come into cohesive community with others. Bakhtin's version, quoted in the title of this book, reads: "What is it that guarantees the internal connection between the elements of personality? Only the unity of responsibility. For what I have experienced and understood, I answer with my life" (in Morson, p. x).

Intellectuals, Organizations, Institutions, and the State

If becoming political is a *human* activity, then no one has a monopoly on thinking/acting politically. Furthermore, those who are not "professional" philosophers-politicians have a specific, inimitable contribution to make: "the real development of the revolutionary process occurs below the surface, in the obscurity of the factory and the obscurity of the consciousness of the numberless masses whom capitalism subjects to its laws" (Gramsci, p. xxxix). Authored in the obscurity of nameless educational institutions, the life histories of these few women remind us of the extraordinary theoretical and practical powers of *ordinary* teachers and their students.

For these activist teachers, and for their students, educational institutions are not mechanisms through which individuals are unconsciously subjected to the dominant ideological system, as in Althusser's ISA (ideological state apparatus); rather, schools are a "terrain on which" they "move, acquire consciousness of their position, struggle, etc." (Gramsci, p. 377). It is, of course, primarily in educational endeavors that these women encounter those *for* whom, *with* whom, and *against* whom they work. And it is through their educational-political practice that they develop the relationship to those around them which Gramsci calls "the organic intellectual."

However difficult or easy its acquisition, these women do bring the privilege of their own education to their relationship with their students; whatever one calls this advantage, "cultural capital," "professional credentials," "social class status," or "analytical skills," these teachers do possess certain intellectual assets which their students do not. What is absolutely critical to this relationship, however, is not what they *have*, but *how*, and *for whom*, they use it.

If these narrators can be said to have any *habitus*, it would have to be defined as a "disposition to empathy." Whether they have developed their "listening heart" as a result of their own oppressive childhood experiences, on account of their own humiliating experiences as a teacher, because of a perceived disparity between their own privilege and the deprivation of others, and/or in association with a sympathic interpretive community, there can be no doubt that these women do hear the voices of those in subordinate social positions, and subsequently join with them "in the practical transformation of the real world" (Gramsci, p. 333).

Although, in some senses, they possess fewer *theoretical* assets than the teachers, the interpellating students also bring essential elements to this relationship; "in their *practical* activity," they present "the principles and the problems" which the organic intellectual must "work out and make coherent." The politically progressive educator can "never forget to remain in contact" with those in subordinate social positions, for it is here that she finds the sources of the problems she "sets out to study and resolve" (Gramsci, p. 330); the relationship between the teacher and the student, or the intellectual and her people, should be as theory is to practice.

These teachers and their students develop the principles and practices of their particular pedagogies, not according to abstract definitions of external theories, nor according to the narrow strictures of local regulations, but in political partnership. The relationship between the teacher and the student is *active and reciprocal,*" because "every teacher is always a pupil and every pupil a teacher" (Gramsci, p. 350); it is *personal,* because it is "an encounter between two human beings" (Huebner, 1985); and it is *political,* because it is part of a larger collective process. As the students become more aware and more organized, so does the teacher; it is in this *process* that she is constituted as an organic intellectual of a particular historical group.

"The process of creating intellectuals is long, difficult, full of contradictions, advances and retreats, dispersals and regroupings," writes Gramsci (p. 334). As the progressive teacher increases her participation and collaboration in the development of the political project, her pedagogic intentions become increasingly incongruent with the prevailing objectives of the educational institution, and she must continually (re)position herself inside (or outside) of the established (public or parochial) school system (Casey, 1992). At the same time, institutional arrangements themselves shift under the pressure of historical events. So, as these women and their associates struggle "systematically and patiently" to form, develop, and render themselves and those with whom they work "ever more homogeneous, compact, and self-aware" (Gramsci, p. 185), their organizational maneuvers and arrangements are widely varied and constantly changing.

That these contingencies and complexities can be disregarded tells us more about the inadequacies of particular assessors than it does about the objects of their criticism. "There exists a scholastic and academic historio-political outlook," writes Gramsci (p. 200) disapprovingly,

> which sees as real and worthwhile only such movements of revolt as are one hundred per cent conscious, i.e., movements that are governed by plans worked out in advance to the last detail or in line with abstract theory (which comes to the same thing).

It is from such a mistaken perspective that efforts such as those presented here are regularly (and in my estimation, wrongly) depreciated as partial, temporary, and inadequate.

I do not claim that any of the organizations which these women create, and within which they participate, are sufficiently widespread and enduring to be recognized as a political "party." Yet while Gramsci (p. 335) does stress "the importance and significance" of the political party "in the elaboration and diffusion of conceptions of the world," he never restricts the terrain of political struggle to the state. Quite the reverse, insisting on historically responsive strategies, Gramsci emphasizes the indispensible contribution of various forms of political organizing. Indeed, the small-scale, local coalitions within which these women generally work correspond in meaningful ways to the "factory council movement animated by *Ordine Nuovo*" (Hoare and Smith in Gramsci, p. 202).

Judging from their narratives, these women do not want to devote much of their energy to large, long-established, institutional organizations, even apparently alternative ones. They are wary of male-dominated projects, including teachers' unions. Like most of their contemporaries, they express contempt for politicians, and fear or disgust towards government, an appropriate response considering the last ten years of cynical, self-interested, conservative restructuring of the state. Considering the self-destructive improbity of the Bolshevik project, the notion of "seizing the state" is both improbable and suspect. Of course, none of these examples means that these women refuse to act, but that they choose to become political in specific ways, within particular personal-social relationships.

At various historical moments, these women have experienced "the ecstasy of resistance," "the rare elation of righteous rage"; they have "known moments when doubts and differences are suspended and people come together in a single-minded quest"; they also remember the "harsh aftermath, when the hangover of the heady days is felt" (Schmemann, 1991: 1). It is precisely in their active response to the doldrums of political defeat that the narratives of these teachers are to be especially appreciated. While others may be rendered impotent in such conditions, these women actually increase their efforts to assist those whose suffering is exacerbated by hard times. Seizing not the state itself, but only its social service functions, they feed the hungry, shelter the homeless, and advise the vulnerable.

"Fatalism" is, in Gramsci's (p. 337) words, "clothing worn by real and active will when in a weak position"; he might well be scolding many contemporary academic intellectuals when he writes:

It is essential at all times to demonstrate the futility of mechanical determinism.—When it is adopted as a thought-out and coherent philosophy on the part of the intellectuals, it becomes a cause of passivity, of idiotic self-sufficiency. This happens when they don't even expect that the subaltern will become directive and responsible.

How can we conceive of social change in a time of conservative trium-phalism? Honoring the narratives presented here allows us to recuperate Gramsci's "optimism of the will"; listening to the voices of women working for social change renews our faith in positive progressive "political passion,"

> an immediate impulse to action which is born on the "perma-nent and organic" terrain of economic life but which tran-scends it, bringing into play emotions and aspirations in whose incandescent atmosphere even calculations involving the individ-ual human life itself obey different laws from those of individ-ual profit (Gramsci, p. 140).

Positive Progressive Political Passion

> An historical act can only be performed by "collective [wo]man," and this presumes the attainment of a "cultural-social" unity through which a multiplicity of dispersed wills, with heterogeneous aims, are welded together with a single aim, on the basis of an equal and common conception of the world, both general and particular, operating in transitory bursts (in emotional ways) or permanently (where the intellec-tual base is so well-rooted, assimilated and experienced that it becomes passion). Since this is the way things happen, great im-portance is assumed by the general questions of *language*, that is, the question of collectively attaining a single cultural "cli-mate" (Gramsci, p. 349; emphasis added).

"Even in the most unhappy schools there are certain classes that stand out like little islands of excitement, energy and hope," Kozol writes in *Savage Inequalities* (p. 47); "in the center" of one of these rooms, "within the rocking chair, and cradling a newborn in her arms, is Mrs. Hawkins" (p. 48). When Kozol (pp. 48–49) quotes this teacher's words, I suddenly feel as if I am reading one of my own transcripts:

164

"This woman," Mrs. Hawkins tells me, "is a parent. She
wanted to help me. So I told her, 'If you don't have someone
to keep your baby, bring the baby here. I'll be the mother. I
can do it.' "—
   "This is the point of it," she says. "I'm teaching them three
things. Number one: self-motivation. Number two: self-esteem.
Number three: You help your sister and your brother. I tell
them they're responsible for each other."—"The most important thing for me is that they teach each other."

From the beginning of this analysis, I have drawn attention to the
ways in which "language is a site of political activity" (Newton and
Rosenfelt, 1985: xxi). Understood in light of that exposition, the metaphor of teacher-as-mother which emerges from Mrs. Corla Hawkins'
conversation (quoted above) takes on enormous *political* significance.
Here, it would seem, is another teacher whose concerns do not coincide
with the military-industrial logic of the national reports on education;
here is another example of "an immediate impulse to action" which
obeys "different laws from those of individual profit" (Gramsci, p.
140); here is another woman who hears the voices of poor black
children, and answers with her life.
   The discursive contribution of ordinary teachers working for social
change cannot be dismissed as merely individual or simply subjective,
for these women theorize in active and reciprocal relationships, as
members of an interpretive community, and as part of a living tradition.
Of course, "a new symbolic mode is not *all* we need" (Newton and
Rosenfelt, 1985: xx). But the particular understandings of the world
which these women express in their discourses has been conceived
in political practice. Not only do these women (re)create distinctive
concepts and metaphors; they (re)produce particular forms of social
relations, and they (re)construct specific dimensions of the social environment; they change their own lives and the lives of those with whom
they work.
   New social languages for valuing education are presented in these
narratives; and new worldviews, grounded in innovative educational
and political projects, are revealed. As they tell the story of their own
lives, these women are meaning-makers; they are authors of whole
new volumes of social text. It is in all these senses that the women in
this study have become "authors"—in the creation and recreation
of social meaning through their educational, political, and narrative
practices.
   While we may now want to incorporate the metaphors created by

these teachers into the larger critical discourse, we must remember that they are not just poetic fancies. These worldviews have been created, and will continue to be recreated, as part of moral and material, political and practical struggles of particular women teachers in their every day lives. In this sense, they cannot be separated from the contexts in which they originated, any more than the schools which these women created could be transplanted to another site. They are part of the whole social web to which these women belong and within which they have worked.

"I give myself shape," writes Bakhtin (in Clark and Holquist, p. 214), "ultimately from the point of view of the community to which I belong." But he continues, "A word is a bridge thrown between myself and another . . . it is territory shared by both addresser and addressee." It is precisely because all educational and political actions must be grounded in some particular social environment, that they must also be different from each other. An analysis of these narratives discloses diverse political projects; but it also demonstrates their social inclusivity; and it reveals their progressive points of convergence. All educators working for social change have a great deal to learn from the care these women give to their students; the outrage they feel towards injustice, and the way they dare to use the limited power that they have.

There is, according to Bakhtin (in Morson, 1986, p. ix), no last word, "only the penultimate word," which "places after itself only a conditional, not a final period." In a similar mood, one of the women in this study remarks, "the world is bigger than the book." In this spirit, I close this work only to open for its readers all the educational and political possibilities it may inspire.

Notes

1. I am indebted to Makeba Casey for the words to this anarchistic children's song. The complete text is:

   Deck the halls with gasoline,
   Fa la la la la la la la la;
   Light a match and watch them gleam,
   Fa la la la la la la la la;
   Watch the schoolhouse burn to ashes,
   Fa la la la la la la la la;
   Aren't you glad you played with matches,
   Fa la la la la la la la la.

2. These three quotations, taken from life history narratives of women teachers who participated in this study, reappear in later chapters. The italics in this and other direct quotations from the narratives are used to indicate a particularly strong emphasis in the speaker's voice.

3. I discuss the national reports on education at some length elsewhere (Casey, 1988a). I am indebted to a number of excellent critical analyses for my understanding of these texts. See, for example, Altbach's description of "who's who" in the national commissions on education, Slaughter's evidence on the exploitation of racial fears, and Spring's delineation of the various interest groups involved, in Altbach, *et al.* (1985). Also see Brosio's (1987) political analysis, and Cinnamond's (1987) metaphorical

deconstruction. The political relations of production of *A Nation at Risk* are revealed in Olson (1988), and Debate (1988).

4. The political life of teachers, when not completely ignored, has been narrowly defined and inconclusively appraised. Teachers have been variously portrayed as conservative (Lortie, 1975), as reproducers of the structures of inequality (Rist, 1970), as victims of the structures of inequality (Spencer, 1986), or as potential actors in connection with unions (Lieberman, 1956). Progressive scholars are, all too often, inclined to hortatory declamation on, rather than empirical investigation of, this subject.

    There are some exceptions; Sterling (1972), for example, presents profiles of "socially conscious inner-city teachers" in the sixties; Apple (1984) notes local mobilizations of progressive teachers' groups; the Boston Women Teachers' Group (1983) conducts research on its members' working conditions; Connell (1985), Weiler (1988), and Middleton (1987, 1989) analyze interviews with feminist teachers; Grumet (1987), Miller (1988), Krall (1988), Ellsworth (1989), Lather (1991) and others have written autobiographical accounts of their own experiences as feminist educators.

5. For a scholarly discussion of teacher-as-worker and teacher-as-female-worker, see Casey and Apple (1989). For an academic discussion of teacher-as-mother, see Casey (1990b).

6. For more detailed criticisms of academic research on teachers, see Casey and Apple (1989), Casey (1990b) and Casey (1992).

7. See, for example, Gottschalk, 1951; Boocock, 1978; Grele, 1978; and Thompson, 1978.

8. In a study of American values, Bellah, *et al.* (1985, p. 219) observe that "although we seldom asked specially about religion, time and again in our conversations, religion emerged as important to the people we were interviewing."

9. There is not only a general public disregard of the history of religious women's work; this is also a neglected area of academic research. Sr. Elizabeth Kolmer (1980) observes: "Although Catholic sisters have been active on the American scene since the eighteenth century, the story of their life and work remains largely untold. Significant opportunities exist for serious researchers in this untouched area of social history."

10. Kolmer (1980) remarks several times on the homogeneity of American Catholic sisters as a social group.

11. I am indebted to West (1982) for the key words used in this particular description of the constituent elements of a discourse.

12. In the sections on "defining the self," I am indebted to Christ's (1980)

discussion of women's religious experience for the general movement of my argument, as well as for those particular phrases which will be noted.

13. The departure of large numbers of women from religious congregations in the past twenty years can be partially explained by the radical changes in these institutions during those years. It appears that identities and contexts fell out of synchronization for these women. I will not attempt to discuss this trend here, nor to establish any general relationship between changes in institutions and changes in individual identities. The one woman in this study who had left the convent gave as one of her reasons the fact that she was ahead of her time, and wished to do things which her order was not ready to allow. But another woman who is still a nun did not wait for her order to change; she instigated innovations. For many women, personal and institutional change seem to have occurred simultaneously, e.g., "Not only am I a transition person as far as the changes that have happened to me in the religious life, but I am in transition in myself.

14. A teacher who read an early draft of this chapter commented: "My principal did not go to the funeral of a teacher at our school who died of AIDS; he simply asked if we 'were well represented.' "

15. Some of the awkwardness of this terminology comes from my attempts to circumnavigate the strong ideological currents around this word. To speak of a "literal" versus a "symbolic" family is to give precedence to a particular construction of family as more "real." I am trying to argue that all "families" are socially constructed realities, having moral and material dimensions.

16. By using the term "interpellation," I enter a particular part of the debate on the nature of subjectivity. I find the metaphor of "summoning" very useful, but I disagree with Althusser's (1972) characterization of subjects as solely the creations of discourse. In my view, they are also its creators.

17. I enter another part of the debate on the nature of subjectivity by using the word "habitus." I find the implications of this metaphor (abiding in ideology) extremely helpful, but I use it to describe the conscious and active role of a subject *vis-à-vis* her own "dispositions," in contrast to the unconscious, reproductive emphasis in Bourdieu (1971).

18. In *Power on the Left: American Radical Movements since 1946,* Lader (1979: ix) also argues that "the Left in recent decades has been essentially pragmatic, nurtured by American needs and not by a closed system imposed from abroad. The Left has generally aimed at limited goals, not cataclysmic revolution. And it has been highly fragmented."

19. Brenner (1986: 56) notes: "Individual Jews . . . will always play a role in the socialist struggle. However, these individuals will not amount to

a majority of Jews. We have no reason to be surprised at this because Jews are now, on average, the richest ethnic group in this country. Class illusions and interests usually immunize upper- and middle-class youth against the revolutionary message." While I do not accept such categories as "individuals" and "illusions," I do agree with the thrust of Brenner's argument, that conservative as well as progressive political positions can be constructed around Jewish identity.

20. For a basic formulation of these concepts, I have referred to Petrovic's (1983: 384–389) short piece on "Praxis," in *A Dictionary of Marxist Thought.* Of course, there have been debates about the meaning of these terms among Marxists; see pages 386–387 in Petrovic in particular. In my discussion, I will simply explicate the implicit definitions used in *these* narratives.

21. Due to its sexist language, I have adapted, rather than quoted, word for word, Petrovic's (1983: 384) definition of "praxis": "free, universal, creative and self-creative activity through which man creates (makes, produces) and changes (shapes) his historical, human world and himself."

22. I am indebted to William H. Sewell's (1980) *Work and Revolution in France: The Language of Labor from the Old Regime to 1848* for the phrase "language of labor." Sewell's theoretical assumptions, analytical methods, and political position, I have discovered, fundamentally correspond to my own, but my work would have been immeasurably weaker without access to his. Although it is based upon a different period of history, his book has served as an important inspiration for my analysis in this chapter.

23. For works which stress proletarianization, deskilling and unionizing of teachers' work, see, for example, Lieberman, 1956, Apple, 1982, Urban, 1982, and Carlson, 1986.

24. For works which suggest a metaphor of "craft" in connection with education, see, for example, Popkewitz, 1972, 1977, Zeichner, 1983, and Tom, 1984.

25. In a remarkable replication of this reminiscence, another white woman (not in this group) who was teaching in California at the time of George Jackson's death, showed me a memorial card from his funeral. She had saved it for twenty years.

    George Jackson (1941–1971), black revolutionary writer, "entered prison at age 15 to serve a sentence of one year to life for stealing $70 from a gas station. He spent the rest of his life in prison, including seven and a half years in solitary confinement" (Low and Cliffe, 1981). According to prison authorities, Jackson was killed by prison guards during an escape attempt.

    As these two narratives attest, Jackson's books (*Soledad Brother: The*

Prison Letters of George Jackson and *Blood in my Eye*) had tremendous influence on white radicals in the seventies.

26. In the opening pages of this chapter, and elsewhere in the book, I employ the racial adjective "black." Of course, there never can be an umproblematic usage of such vocabulary. My problem here is part of a larger debate; see, for example, the discussion of bracketing the word "race" in *"Race," Writing and Difference* (Gates, 1986).

Two specific points need to be made in this regard: (1) I am very conscious of the essentializing powers of this racial naming, and simply mean to *postpone* discussion of its social construction, which is a central issue in my analysis of these teachers' narratives; (2) I have chosen to retain the self-naming employed by these women *at the time of their interviews,* not to adjust my usage to subsequent changes in the vocabulary of race.

27. By linking the two, I assert that ethnicity and race share important common characteristics.

Throughout the seventies and eighties, there was no scholarly consensus on definitions of ethnicity and race. Banks' (1979: 5) formulation suggests that ethnicity is *something you are:* "An ethnic group is an involuntary group which shares a heritage, kinship ties, a sense of identification, political and economic interests, and cultural and linguistic characteristics"; Schermerhorn's (1979: 12), *something you have:* "An ethnic group is defined here as a collectivity within a larger society having a real or putative common ancestry, memories of a shared past, and a cultural focus on one or more symbolic elements defined as the epitome of their peoplehood"; Cohen's (1981: 308), *something you use:* "An ethnic group is a collectivity of people who share some interests in common, and who, in interaction with other collectivities, coordinate their activities in advancing and defending these interests by means of a communal type of organization, manipulating in the process such cultural forms as kinship, myths of origin, and rites and ceremonies;" Yancey, *et al.* (1976: 391) argue that ethnicity is *a continual process of becoming:* "Rather than a constant ascribed trait that is inherited from the past, ethnicity is the result of a process which continues to unfold. It is basically a manifestation of the way populations are organized in terms of interaction patterns, institutions, personal values, attitudes, life styles and presumed consciousness of kind."

The divergent definitions in educational policy statements represent different political agendas. Ethnicity and race are presented as "problems" needing "professional management" in such liberal proposals as Orfield's (1978) recommendations of money, expertise, and leadership for desegregation and Baker's (1977) arguments for multicultural teacher education. The many formulations which reduce ethnicity/race to the individual (e.g., James, 1980), to the cultural (e.g., Hale, 1981), or to the psychological (e.g., Glazer, 1981), reinforce the status quo by ignoring economic and political conflicts. Definitions of ethnicity and race as private (e.g., Isaacs, 1981) or nonpolitical matters (e.g., Clark in Hentoff, 1982) serve conservative or reactionary interests, because in a situation of inequality, universalistic criterion work to the advantage of the privileged. More progressive formulations see ethnicity/race as collective, conflictual, and changing, as political and economic phenomena (Barth and Noel, 1972; Cohen, 1981; Wax, 1972).

While in light of the role of the slave narrative tradition in my analysis, Omi and Winant's (1986: 68–69) emphasis on race as "*an unstable and 'decentered' complex of social meanings constantly being transformed by political struggle*" seems to overemphasize change, their statement of purpose does convey the intentions of this book.

The crucial task . . . is to suggest how the widely disparate circumstances of individual and group racial identities, and of the racial institutions and social practices with which these identities are intertwined, are formed and transformed over time. This takes place . . . through *political contestation over racial meanings* (emphasis in original).

28. The papers presented at the symposium, *Capturing the Black Teacher's Voice*, at the AERA Annual Meeting, Boston, Massachusetts, 1990, were: Michele Foster (1990a), "Black teachers and the politics of race"; Annette Henry, "Black women/Black pedagogies: An African Canadian context"; Etta Ruth Hollins, "Reexamination of what works for inner city Black children"; Gloria Ladson-Billings, "Making a little magic: Teachers' talk about successful teaching strategies for Black children." The chair was Joyce King; the discussants, Beverly Gordon and Paul Ramsey. Articles based on these papers appeared in the *Journal of Education:* see Foster (1990b), Gordon (1990), King and Wilson (1990), Ladson-Billings and Henry (1990), Hollins and Spencer (1990), and others, in volume 172, numbers 2 and 3. Also see Foster (1991).

29. According to Watkins' (1991) typology of African-American curriculum theories, the women in this study are not black nationalists; they are reconstructionists.

30. After all, among the women in this group who grew up in the South, one lived in small-town North Carolina, one in rural Mississippi, and one in urban New Orleans; the fourth woman's childhood was spent in a large northeastern city. Other potentially important variations include teaching predominantly black, predominantly white, or racially mixed groups of children; teaching at preschool, elementary or high school levels; mar-

rying black men (three women) or a white man (one woman), being divorced (two women). The researcher could also choose to categorize these women according to a spectrum of color among persons called "black".

Concerning these and other issues of difference among the women, I have taken decisions on the same basis as with other groups: (1) I primarily attend to those items which the narrators themselves emphasize, and (2) I structure my discussion around *commonalities* among the narratives.

31. Throughout this chapter, I deliberately alternate the word *slave* with other phrases which dislodge any notion of white-property-rights-over-black-human-beings from that name. I am indebted to my student, Daniel Huff, for calling to my attention the phrase "human beings held in bondage." McLaughlin (1990: xlvii) takes the phrases "kidnapped African" and "daughter of captivity," from an article by Harris.

32. In "Men led, but women organized: Movement participation of women in the Mississippi Delta," Payne (1990: 10) presents an historian's version of this same point:

It has traditionally been a black-majority country, which is not unusual for the Delta, but since before World War II it has also been a country in which most of the land has been owned by blacks. It is almost certain landownership gives them a greater degree of freedom from economic reprisals, but one student of the county's history feels that the tradition of landownership and cooperative work contributed to a distinctive worldview among the men. Salamon found that compared to local sharecroppers, the landowners were more optimistic about the future, had a higher sense of personal efficacy, and were more likely to feel that they had been of help to others. By every measure, landowners were far more likely to participate in the early civil rights movement. Thus it may be that landowning for men, perhaps especially when blacks own whole communities, has some of the same psychological effects as religion for women, particularly with respect to an enhanced sense of personal efficacy.

33. I am indebted to Braxton (1989: 211) for her clear definition of this naming:

I use the term *Afra-American* (as an adjective) to designate the distinctively feminine aspects of black American literature and culture; the term is, by definition, feminist, or to use the word coined by Alice Walker, 'womanist,' in that it places the experience of black women at the center and speaks from that perspective. Neither race nor gender is privileged;

173

a united and integrated view is expressed. The speaker is neither a black who happens to be a woman nor a woman who happens to be a black, but is an individual whose perspective encompasses the multiple elements of a complex identity.

Her words are echoed by one of the black women teachers:

If I had to decide right now if I have been discriminated against more because I am a woman, or more because I am a black, I would not be able to tell you. And, it's just like, what came first, the chicken or the egg. OK? And I kind of put a lot of black people off when I say that, but I'm prepared to defend it, you know. There are days when I feel more pressed as a woman. And there are days I feel more pressed as a black. You know. And there are times when, if the oppression is coming from someone who is really very close to you, and it happens to be a someone of the opposite sex, that you *really* feel oppressed.

34. Here I use Gramsci's (1980) notion of the *organic intellectual*, understood as a thinker who is both *of* and *for* a particular social group. The metaphor of geneology is used here to describe the creation of political ancestors and descendants, with particular reference to the African-American interpretive community.

35. Gender battles *within* the black family/community (McDowell, 1989) are not an elaborated theme in these narratives.

36. This section is dependent upon Bakhtin's definition of "carnival," and, especially on Clark and Holquist's (1984) explication of that notion, as indicated in various citations.

37. I use parentheses here to enclose descriptors which the narrator herself does not use, but which are, in my estimation, essential to the reader's understanding of the episode under discussion. It is quite extraordinary to realize that this speaker describes the people involved in this particular event without resorting to adjectives of color. Elsewhere in her interview, she emphatically states: "I am pro-black; I'm not anti-anything."

38. I am not entirely comfortable with the political label "progressive," mistakenly understood by at least one early reader as referring to the "Progressive Era." Yet it has some usefulness as an overarching and inclusive term for anti-conservative political projects. I also use the word "left" (with a lower-case "l") in this section as an antonym of "right," and a synonym of "progressive"; this is different from the label "Left" (with an upper-case "L") in chapter five, which refers to identifiably Marxist and neo-Marxist projects. I add "(s)" in the same sense as Lather (1991: xv) writes about "feminism(s)" and "neo-Marxism(s)," to indicate multiplicity of theories/practices within the largest category, as

well as within its various historical "parts." I explore the relationship of these "parts" to the "whole" in the discussion which follows.

39. The reconceptualization of Marxist theorizing in Johnson's (1980; 1981) *problematic* resonates with Gramsci's (p. 324) proposition: "one's conception of the world is a response to certain *specific* problems posed by reality, which are quite specific and '*original*' in their *immediate* relevance" (emphasis added). So does the Popular Memory Group's (1982: 225) argument that "major shifts (in methodology) are . . . likely to arise from changes in political or theoretical preoccupations induced by social events."

Among meta-theoretical analyses dependent on Gramsci, a variation of Johnson's (1980: 202) assertion that "elements taken from different existing problematics may, in a new order, and constituting a new field, yield us greater explanatory power and political purchase" appears in Laclau and Mouffe's (1985: 5) argument that "the discourses that constitute the field of classical Marxism may help to form the thinking of a new left by bequesting some of their concepts, transforming or abandoning others, and diluting themselves in that infinite intertextuality of emancipatory discourses in which the plurality of the social takes shape." In another version, Gouldner (1985: 203) emphasizes that, in Marx's *own* work, "the simultaneous presence of multiple intellectual traditions . . . constituted a new symbolic context, a *re*-contextualization, of each of the constituent traditions, endowing each with a changed interpretation and novel meaning." There are other scholars too numerous to mention who find Gramsci's work an indispensible resource.

Of course I am myself not only indebted to Gramsci, but also to those interpreters who have assisted my reading of his work. I am particularly indebted to Michael Burawoy's course in Twentieth Century Marxism, offered in Spring 1983 at the University of Wisconsin-Madison. Seen from another angle, the apparently eclectic assembly of other theorists which I cite throughout this book all exhibit some coincidence with the conceptual configuration so comprehensively articulated by Gramsci; what is particularly compelling about Gramsci's version is the intensity of his political commitment.

References

Altbach, P. 1985. "The great education 'crisis.' " In Altbach, P., Kelly, G. and Weis, L., ed. *Excellence in Education: Perspectives on Policy and Practice*. Buffalo: Prometheus Books.

Althusser, L. 1972. *Lenin and Philosophy and Other Essays*. Trans. B. Brewster. New York: Monthly Review Press.

Angelou, M. 1990. *I shall Not be Moved*. New York: Random House.

Apple, M. W. 1982. *Education and Power*. Boston: Routledge and Kegan Paul.

———. 1984. "Teaching and 'women's work.' " In E. Gumbert, ed. *Expressions of Power in Education: Studies of Class, Gender, and Race*. Atlanta: Center for Cross-cultural Education, Georgia State University.

Ashcroft, B., Griffiths, G. and Tiffin, H. 1989. *The Empire Writes Back: Theory and Practice in Post-Colonial Literatures*. New York: Routledge.

Baker, G. 1977. "Multicultural imperatives for curriculum development in teacher education." *Journal of Research and Development in Education* II (Fall): 70–83.

Bakhtin, M. M. 1981. *The Dialogic Imagination*. Holquist, M., ed. Emerson, C. and Holquist, M., trans. Austin: University of Texas Press.

Ball, S. J. and Goodson, I., eds. 1985. *Teachers' Lives and Careers*. London: Falmer.

Banks, J. 1979. "Multiethnic/multicultural teacher education: Conceptual, historical, and ideological issues." Paper presented at the American Association of Colleges of Teacher Education, Institute on Multiethnic Studies for Teacher Education, Dallas, Texas (8–10 February).

Barth, E. and Noel, D. 1972. "Conceptual frameworks for the analysis of race relations: An evaluation." *Social Forces* 50 (March): 333–348.

Baruch, G., Barnett, R. and Rivers, C. 1981. "All grown up!" *Ladies Home Journal* (May): 99–181.

Bellah, R., Madsen, R., Sullivan, W., Swidler, A. and Tipton, S. 1985. *Habits of the Heart: Individualism and Commitment in American Life.* New York: Harper and Row.

Benston, K. 1984. "I yam what I am: the topos of (un)naming in Afro-American literature." In Gates, H. L., Jr., ed. *Black Literature and Literary Theory.* New York: Methuen.

Bertaux, D., ed. 1981. *Biography and Society.* Beverly Hills: Sage.

———. 1983. "Letter to the I. S. A. Secretariat." *Biography and Society: Newsletter of the Working Group on the Life History Approach in the Social Sciences* (April): 8–11.

Bladow, J. 1981. "Where are they now?" *Working Women* (July): 57–60.

Boocock, S. S. 1978. "Historical and sociological research on the family and the life cycle: Methodological alternatives." In Demos, J. and Boocock, S., eds. *Turning Points: Historical and Sociological Essays on the Family.* Chicago: University of Chicago Press.

Boston, Women's Teachers' Group. 1983. "The other end of the corridor: The effect of teaching on teachers." *Radical Teacher* 23: 2–23.

Bourdieu, P. 1971. "Intellectual field and creative project." In M. F. D. Young, ed. *Knowledge and Control: New Directions for the Sociology of Education.* London: Collier Macmillan.

Bowles, S. and Gintis, H. 1976. *Schooling in Capitalist America.* New York: Basic Books.

Braxton, J. 1989. *Black Women Writing Autobiography: A Tradition Within a Tradition.* Philadelphia: Temple University Press.

Brenner, L. 1986. *Jews in America Today.* Secaucus: Lyle Stuart.

Brent, L. 1973. *Incidents in the Life of a Slave Girl.* New York: Harcourt Brace Jovanovich.

Brosio, R. 1987. "The present economic sea changes and the corresponding consequences for education." *Educational Foundations,* 3 (Fall): 4–38.

Byerman, K. 1985. *Fingering the Jagged Grain: Tradition and Form in Recent Black Fiction.* Athens and London: University of Georgia Press.

Carby, H. 1987. *Reconstructing Womanhood: The Emergence of the Afro-American Woman Novelist.* New York: Oxford University Press.

Carlson, D. 1987. "Teachers as political actors: From reproductive theory to the crisis of schooling." *Harvard Educational Review* 57, 3 (August): 283–307.

Casey, K. 1987. "Why do progressive women activists leave teaching?" Paper presented at the Annual Meeting of the American Educational Research Association, Washington, D.C.

———. 1988a. *Teacher as Author: Life History Narratives of Contemporary Women Teachers Working for Social Change.* Ph.D. dissertation. University of Wisconsin-Madison.

———. 1988b. "Race, gender and class in the life history narratives of black women teachers." Paper presented at the Annual Meeting of the American Educational Research Association, Washington, D.C.

———. 1988c. "Varieties of feminism in the life history narratives of contemporary women teachers." Paper presented at National Women's Studies Association Annual Meeting, Minneapolis, MN.

———. and Laird, S. 1989. "Concepts and narratives: The 'mother' problem in feminism and education." Paper presented at Bergamo Conference on Curriculum Theory and Practice.

———. 1990a. "Teachers as curriculum theorists: Generating new definitions of nurture in education." Paper presented at the Annual Meeting of the American Educational Research Association, Boston, MA.

———. 1990b. "Teacher as mother: Curriculum theorizing in the life histories of contemporary women teachers." *Cambridge Journal of Education* 20, 3: 301–320.

———. 1992. "Why do progressive women activists leave teaching? Theory, methodology and politics in life history research." In Goodson, I., ed. *Studying Teachers' Lives.* London: Routledge.

———. and Apple, M. 1989. "Gender and the condition of teachers' work: The development of understanding in America. In Acker, S., ed. *Teachers, Gender and Careers.* New York and London: Falmer Press.

Christ, C. 1980. *Diving Deep and Surfacing: Women Writers on Spiritual Quest.* Boston: Beacon Press.

Christian, B. 1985. *Black Feminist Criticism: Perspectives on Black Women Writers.* New York: Pergamon.

Cinnamond, J. 1987. "Metaphors as understanding: Recent reform reports on education." Paper presented at the meeting of the Association for the Study of Higher Education, San Diego, CA. (ERIC document ED 281 439.)

Clark, K. and Holquist, M. 1984. *Mikhail Bakhtin.* Cambridge: Harvard University Press.

Cohen, A. 1981. "Variables in ethnicity." In Keynes, C., ed. *Ethnic Change.* Seattle: University of Washington Press.

Collins, P. H. 1989. "The social construction of black feminist thought." *Signs* 14, 4: 745–773.

Connell, R. W. 1985. *Teachers' Work.* Sydney: George Allen and Unwin.

Crawford, V. 1990. "Beyond the human self: Grassroots activists in the Mississippi Civil Rights Movement." In Crawford, V., Rouse, J. A. and Woods, B., eds. *Women in the Civil Rights Movement: Trailblazers and Torchbearers, 1941–1965.* Brooklyn, N.Y.: Carlson Publishing Company.

Davis, F. 1979. *Yearning for Yesterday.* New York: The Free Press.

"Debate over report's tenor lasted to the final months." 1988. *Education Week* 7, 31 (April 27): 22.

DeCamargo, A. 1981. "The actor and the system." In Bertaux, D., ed. *Biography and Society.*

Dreeben, R. 1970. *The Nature of Teaching: School and the Work of Teachers.* Glenview, Illinois: Scott, Foreman and Company.

DuBois, W.E.B. (1903). 1965. *The Souls of Black Folk.* Reprinted in *Three Negro Classics.* New York: Avon.

Elder, G. 1977. *Children of the Great Depression: Social Change in Life Experience.* Chicago: University of Chicago Press.

———. 1981. "History and life course." In Bertaux, D., ed. *Biography and Society.*

Ellison, Ralph. 1972. *Invisible Man.* New York: Vintage Books.

Ellsworth, E. 1989. "Why doesn't this feel empowering? Working through the repressive myths of critical pedagogy." *Harvard Educational Review* 59, 3 (August): 297–324.

Evans, S. 1980. *Personal Politics: The Roots of Women's Liberation in the Civil Rights Movement and the New Left.* New York: Vintage.

Ferrarotti, F. 1981. "On the autonomy of the biographical method." In Bertaux, D., editor. *Biography and Society.*

Fiorenza, E. S. 1985. *In Memory of Her: A Feminist Theological Reconstruction of Christian Origins.* New York: Crossroads.

Fish, S. 1980. *Is There a Text in This Class? The Authority of Interpretive Communities.* Cambridge: Harvard University Press.

Fordham, S. 1988. "Racelessness as a factor in Black students' school success: Pragmatic strategy or pyrrhic victory?" *Harvard Educational Review* 58, 1 (February): 54–84.

Foster, M. 1990a. "Black teachers and the politics of race." Paper presented at the Annual Meeting of the American Educational Research Association, Boston, MA.

———. 1990b. "The politics of race: Through the eyes of African-American teachers." *Journal of Education* 172, 3: 123–141.

————. 1991. "Constancy, connectedness, and constraints in the lives of African-American teachers." *NWSA Journal* 3, 2 (Spring): 233–261.

Gates, D. (1940). 1968. *Blue Willow.* New York: Scholastic.

Gates, H. L., Jr. 1984a. "Criticism in the jungle." In Gates, H. L., Jr., ed. *Black Literature and Literary Theory.*

————. 1984b. "The blackness of blackness: A critique of the sign and the signifying monkey." In Gates, H. L., Jr., ed. *Black literature and literary theory.*

————, ed. 1986. *"Race," Writing, and Difference.* Chicago: University of Chicago Press.

————. 1987. *Figures in Black: Words, Signs, and the "Racial" Self.* New York: Oxford University Press.

————. 1988. *The Signifying Monkey: A Theory of African-American Literary Criticism.* New York: Oxford University Press.

————. 1989. "Canon-formation, literary history, and the Afro-American tradition: From the seen to the told." In Houston Baker, H., Jr. and Redmond, P., eds. *Afro-American Literary Study in the 1990s.* Chicago: University of Chicago Press.

Gilligan, C. 1982. *In a Different Voice.* Cambridge, Massachusetts: Harvard University Press.

Giovanni, N. 1975. *The Women and the Men: Poems.* New York: William Morrow and Company.

Glazer, N. 1981. "Ethnicity and education: Some hard questions." *Phi Delta Kappan* 62, 5 (January): 386–389.

Goodson, I. 1992. "Studying teachers' lives: An emergent field of inquiry." In I. Goodson, ed. *Studying Teachers' Lives.* London: Routledge.

Gordon, B. 1990. "The necessity of African-American epistemology for educational theory and practice." *Journal of Education* 172, 3: 88–106.

Gornick, V. 1977. *The Romance of American Communism.* New York: Basic Books.

Gottschalk, L. 1951. "The historian and the historical document." In Gottschalk, L., *et al.*, eds. *The Uses of Personal Documents in History, Anthropology and Sociology.* New York: Social Science Research Council.

Goulder, A. 1985. *Against Fragmentation: The Origins of Marxism and the Sociology of Intellectuals.* Oxford: Oxford University Press.

Graham, P. A. 1987. "Black teachers: A drastically scarce resource." *Phi Delta Kappan* 68, 8 (April): 598–605.

Gramsci, A. 1980. *Selections from the Prison Notebooks of Antonio Gramsci.* Ed. and trans. Q. Hoare and G. N. Smith. New York: International Publishers.

Grele, R. 1978. "Can anyone over thirty be trusted: a friendly critique of oral history." *Oral History Review:* 36–44.

Grumet, M. 1987. "The politics of personal knowledge." *Curriculum Inquiry* 17, 3 (Fall): 320–329.

Hale, J. 1981. "Research in review. Black children: Their roots, culture and learning styles." *Young Children* 36 (January): 37–50.

Henry, A. 1990. "Black women/Black pedagogies: An African Canadian context." Paper presented at the Annual Meeting of the American Educational Research Association, Boston, MA.

Hentoff, N. 1981. "Profiles: The integrationist." *The New Yorker* (August 23): 37–73.

Hirsch, M. 1989. *The Mother/Daughter Plot: Narrative, Psychoanalysis, Feminism.* Bloomington: Indiana University Press.

Hoare, Q. and Smith, G. N. 1980. "Introduction." In Gramsci, A. *Selections from the Prison Notebooks of Antonio Gramsci.*

Hobsbaum, E. 1984. *Workers: Worlds of Labor.* New York: Pantheon.

Hollings, E. R. 1990. "Reexamination of what works for inner-city Black children." Paper presented at the Annual Meeting of the American Educational Research Association, Boston, MA.

Hollings, E. R. and Spencer, K. 1990. "Restructuring schools for cultural inclusion: Changing the schooling process for African American youngsters." *Journal of Education* 172, 2: 89–100.

Huebner, D. 1975. "Curricular language and classroom meanings." In W. Pinar, ed. *Curriculum Theorizing: The Reconceptualists.* Berkeley: McCutchan.

Holquist, M. 1981. "Introduction." In Bakhtin, M. M. *The Dialogic Imagination.*

Isaacs, H. 1981. "The one and the many." In Yarmolinsky, A., Liebman, L. and Schelling, C., eds. *Race and schooling in the city.* Cambridge: Harvard University Press.

James, R. 1980. "The multicultural teacher education standard—Challenge and opportunity." *Viewpoints in Teaching and Learning* 56 (Winter): 18–25.

Johnson, B. E. 1989. "Response." In Baker, H., Jr. and Redmond, P., eds. *Afro-American Literary Study in the 1990s.*

Johnson, R. 1980. "Three problematics: Elements of a theory of working class culture." In Clarke, J., Cricher, C. and Johnson, R., eds. *Working Class Culture.* London: St. Martins.

———. 1981. "Against absolutism." In Samuel, R., ed. *People's History and Socialist Theory.* London: Routledge and Kegan Paul.

Kemple, J. 1989. "The career paths of black teachers: Evidence from North

Carolina." Paper presented at the Annual Meeting of the American Educational Research Association, San Francisco, CA.

King, J. E. and Wilson, T. L. 1990. "Being a soul-freeing substance: A legacy of hope in Afro-Humanity." *Journal of Education* 172, 2: 9–27.

Kliebard H. 1975. "Metaphorical roots of curriculum design." In Pinar, W., ed. *Curriculum Theorizing: The Reconceptualists*. Berkeley: McCutchan.

Kolmer, Sr. E. 1980. "Catholic women religious and women's history." In James, J. W., ed. *Women in American Religion*. Philadelphia: University of Pennsylvania Press.

Kozol, J. 1967. *Death at an Early Age: The Destruction of the Hearts and Minds of Negro Children in the Boston Public Schools*. New York: Houghton.

———. 1988. *Rachel and Her Children: Homeless Families in America*. New York: Crown Publishers.

———. 1991. *Savage Inequalities: Children in America's Schools*. New York: Crown Publishers.

Krall, F. 1988. "Behind the chairperson's door: Reconceptualizing women's work." In W. Pinar, ed. *Contemporary Curriculum Discourses*. Scottsdale, AZ: Gorsuch Scarisbrick.

Laclau, E. and Mouffe, C. 1985. *Hegemony and Socialist Strategy: Towards a Radical Democratic Politics*. Trans. W. Moore and P. Cammack. London: Verso.

Lader, L. 1979. *Power on the Left: American Radical Movements Since 1946*. New York: W. W. Norton.

Ladson-Billings, G. 1990. "Making a little magic: Teachers' talk about successful teaching strategies for Black children." Paper presented at the Annual Meeting of the American Educational Research Association, Boston, MA.

——— and Henry, A. 1990. "Blurring the borders: Voices of African liberatory pedagogy in the United States and Canada." *Journal of Education* 172, 2: 72, 88.

Lather, P. 1991. *Getting Smart: Feminist Research and Pedagogy With/In the Postmodern*. New York: Routledge.

Lieberman, M. 1956. *Education as a Profession*. Englewood Cliffs, New Jersey: Prentice Hall.

Lortie, D. 1975. *Schoolteacher: A Sociological Study*. Chicago: University of Chicago Press.

Low, W. A. and Cliffe, V. 1981. *Encyclopedia of Black America*. New York: McGraw Hill.

McDowell, D. E. 1989. "Boundaries: Or distant relations and close kin." In Baker, H., Jr. and Redmond, P., eds. *Afro-American Literary Study in the 1990s*.

McFadden, G. J. 1980. *Oral Recollections of Septima Poinsette Clark.* Columbia: USC Instructional Services Center.

McLaughlin, A. N. 1990. "A renaissance of the spirit: Black women remaking the universe." In Braxton, J. and McLaughlin, A. N., eds. *Wild Women in the Whirlwind: Afra-American Culture and the Contemporary Literary Renaissance.* New Brunswick: Rutgers University Press.

Melosh, B. 1982. *The Physician's Hand: Work, Culture and Conflict in American Nursing.* Philadelphia: Temple University Press.

Middleton, S. 1987. "Schooling and radicalisation: Life histories of New Zealand feminist teachers." *British Journal of Sociology of Education* 8, 2.

————. 1989. "Educating feminists: A life-history study." In Acker, S., ed. *Teachers, Gender and Careers.*

Miller, J. 1987. *Democracy is in the Streets.* New York: Simon and Schuster.

Miller, J. L. 1988. "The resistence of women academics: An autobiographical account." In W. Pinar, ed. *Contemporary Curriculum Discourses.* Scottsdale, AZ: Gorsuch Scarisbrick.

Morson, G. S. 1986. "Preface: Perhaps Bakhtin." In Morson, G. S. ed, *Bakhtin: Essays and Dialogues on His Work.* Chicago: University of Chicago Press.

Murnane, R. and Schwinden, M. 1988. "Who became certified to teach, and who entered teaching between 1979 and 1985: Evidence from North Carolina." ERIC document ED301559.

National Commission on Excellence in Education. 1983. *A Nation at Risk.* Washington, D.C.: The Commission Supt. of Docs., U.S., G.P.O. distributors.

Newton, J. and Rosenfelt, D. 1985. "Introduction: Towards a materialist-feminist criticism." In Newton, J., and Rosenfelt, D., eds. *Feminist Criticism and Social Change: Sex, Class and Race in Literature and Culture.* New York: Methuen.

Olson, L. 1988. "Inside 'A Nation At Risk': A view from the cutting-room floor." *Education Week* 7, 31 (April 27): 1, 22, 23.

Omi, M. and Winant, H. 1986. *Racial Formation in the United States: From the 1960s to the 1980s.* London: Routledge and Kegan Paul.

Orfield, G. 1978. *Must We Bus? Segregation and National Policy.* Washington, D.C.: Brookings Institute.

Payne, C. 1990. "Men led, but women organized: Movement participation of women in the Mississippi Delta." In Crawford, V., Rouse, J. A. and Woods, B., eds. *Women in the Civil Rights Movement: Trailblazers and Torchbearers, 1941–1965.* Brooklyn, N.Y.: Carlson Publishing Company.

Perkins, L. 1989. "The history of blacks in teaching: Growth and decline within the profession." In Warren D., ed. *American Teachers: Histories of a Profession at Work.* New York: Macmillan.

Peshkin, A. 1988. "In search of subjectivity—One's own." *Educational Researcher* (October): 17–21.

Petrovic, G. 1983. "Praxis." In Bottomore, T., ed. *A Dictionary of Marxist Thought*. Cambridge: Harvard University Press.

Popkewitz, T. 1972. "The craft of study, structure and schooling." *Teachers College Record* 74, 2: 155–165.

———. 1977. "Craft and community as metaphors for social inquiry curriculum." *Educational Theory* 27, 4: 310–321.

Popular Memory Group. 1982. "Popular memory: Theory, politics, method." In Johnson, R., McLennan, G., Schwarz, B. and Sutton, D., eds. *Making Histories*. London: Hutchinson.

Posner, M. 1986. "William Bennett on new teacher salaries, education problems, and the presidency." In *Newsbank*, EDU 92: B12–13.

Quantz, R. A. and O'Connor, T. 1988. "Writing critical ethnography: Dialogue, multivoicedness, and carnival in cultural texts." *Educational Theory* 38 (Winter), 1: 95–109.

Rist, R. 1970. "Student social class and teacher expectations: The self-fulfilling prophesy of ghetto education." *Harvard Educational Review* 40, 3 (August): 411–452.

Schermerhorn, R. A. 1970. *Comparative Ethnic Relations: A Framework for Theory and Research*. New York: Random House.

Sewell, W. H. 1980. *Work and Revolution in France: The Language of Labor from the Old Regime to 1848*. New York: Cambridge University Press.

Simross, L. 1985. "Class of '65." *Capital Times* 3, 15 (July 24): 1–2.

Slaughter, S. 1985. "Main-traveled road or fast track." In Altbach, P., Kelly, G. and Weis, L., eds. *Excellence in Education*.

Soelle, D. 1991. "Education and democracy." Lecture presented at the School of Education, University of North Carolina at Greensboro.

Spencer, D. A. 1986. *Contemporary Women Teachers: Balancing School and Home*. New York: Longmans.

Spring, J. 1985. "Political and economic analysis." In Altbach, P., Kelly, G. and Weis, L., eds. *Excellence in education*.

Sterling, P., compiler and ed. 1972. *The Real Teachers*. New York: Random House.

Sweet Honey in the Rock. 1981. "On childhood." Words from *The Prophet* by K. Gibran. Music by Y. Barnwell. *Breaths*. Flying Fish.

Tewel, K. and Trubowitz, S. 1987. "The minority group teacher: An endangered species." *Urban Education* 22, 3 (October): 355–65.

Thompson, P. 1978. *The Voice of the Past: Oral History*. Oxford: Oxford University Press.

————. 1981. "Life histories and the analysis of social change." In D. Bertaux, ed. *Biography and Society.*

Todorov, T. 1984. *Mikhail Bakhtin: The Dialogic Principle.* W. Godvich, trans. Minneapolis: University of Minnesota Press.

Tom, A. 1984. *Teaching as a Moral Craft.* New York: Longmans.

Urban, W. 1982. *Why Teachers Organized.* Detroit: Wayne State University Press.

Wall, C. 1989. "Introduction." In Wall, C., ed. *Changing Our Own Words: Essays on Criticism, Theory, and Writing by Black Women.* New Brunswick, N.J.: Rutgers University Press.

Warner, S. A. 1963. *Teacher.* New York: Simon and Schuster.

Watkins, W. 1991. "Black curriculum orientations: A typology." Paper presented at the AERA Annual Meeting, Chicago, IL.

Wax, M. 1972. "Cultural pluralism, political power, and ethnic studies." In Kimball, S. and Burnett, J., eds. *Learning and Culture: Proceedings of the 1972 Annual Spring Meeting of the American Ethnological Society.* Seattle: University of Washington Press.

Weiler, K. 1988. *Women Teaching for Change: Gender, Class and Power.* South Hadley, MA: Bergin and Garvey.

West, C. 1982. *Prophesy Deliverance! An Afro-American Revolutionary Christianity.* Philadelphia: Westminster Press.

White, J. 1981. "Beyond autobiography." In Samuel, R., ed. *People's History and Socialist Theory.* London: Routledge and Kegan Paul.

Willis, P. 1977. *Learning to Labour.* New York: Columbia University Press.

Wright, R. 1968. Interview with Fannie Lou Hamer, August 9, 1968, pages 1–2, from the Civil Rights Documentation Project, Moorland-Sprinarn Research Center, Howard University, Washington, D.C.

Yancey, W., Ericksen, E. and Juliani, R. 1976. "Emergent ethnicity: A review and reformulation." *American Sociological Review* 41 (June): 391–403.

Index

Index

bombs, 128, 146

bondage, 147, 173; *see also* captivity, slavery

Bourdieu, Pierre, (habitus), 61–2, 64, 161, 169

Bowles, S. and Gintis, H., 82

brother, 123

Brother, religious, 43

brotherly love, 55

business, 93, 139

Cajun, 119

capitalism, 155, 160

captivity, 114, 148, 152, 173; *see also* bondage, slavery

Capturing the black teacher's voice, 109, 172

care, 47, 65, 149, 160, 165; *see also love, nurture*

carnival, 19, 141–147, 174; defined, 143

Catholic: researcher's identity as, 9, 70; black, 58; Brothers, 43; clergy, 31, 66; discourse, 29–67, 158; Holy Father, 55; nuns, 4, 26–7, 29–67, 107, 168–9; Pope, 36, 40; schools, *see* schools; tradition, 23, 27, 160; women religious, 4, 26–7, 29–67, 107, 168–9

Catholic church, 36, 48; as family, 55; hierarchy, 38–40; organization, 41, 66; racial segregation, 119, traditional language, 32

Catholic Worker, 9

Catholics for a Free Choice, 38

"changing words," 112

Chavez, Cesar, 9

childhood: of narrators, 34–5, 46–50, 65, 75, 113–20, 124, 127–8, 130–1, 153; of their students, 52–4, 95, 100, 136–7, 141–3; of researcher, 8–9

chivalric code, 123

civil rights: agenda, 105; initiatives, 124; movement, 3, 70–1, 81, 83, 90, 150, 152, 173; research projects, 10; struggles, 121

Clark, Septima Poinsette, 129

class, *see* social class

coalitions, 24, 163

cohort analysis, 77–8

collective: anger, 147; initiative, 45; memory, 32; political understanding, 72; project, 130; reinterpretation, 152; subjective, 26; wisdom, 157; (wo)man, 164

collectivities, 152, 160

colleges and universities and, 3, 8, 15, 42, 70, 77–86, 117, 125, 129, 132–5

commodification, 97, 157

common good, 57

communal: life, 32; meaning, 152; ritual, 143, 145

Communist Party, 70–71; metaphors of, 70

communists, 14, 29, 69–70

community: activism, 82–4; black, 124, 142, 145, 152–3, 174; cohesive, 160; defined, 53; faith, 53; gay, 36; interpretive, 26, 161, 142, 145, 165; school, 54; values, 65

communities, religious, 41–44, 49–50, 60, 62–3, 65–6; as box, frame, 62; *see also* congregations, orders

compassion, 51–52

congregations, religious, 29–30, 39, 41–3, 52, 55–6, 168; *see also* communities, religious orders

Congress, (United States), 78–80

Connell, R. W., 25

conservative: college, 70; discourse, 3; Jewish identity, 76, 169–70; people, 83; politics and race, 140; restructuring of state, 163; scholars, 11; teachers as, 10, 16, 168; triumphalism, 5, 155–7, 164

convents, 30–34, 42, 48, 50–1, 64

CORE (Congress of Racial Equality), 83

cotton picking, 113–4, 117

Creole, 119, 123

critical: discourse, 166; reflection, 82; theorists, 91

cultural capital, 157, 161

curriculum, 9, 82, 96–8, 101–5, 125, 149, 151, 172; languages of, 19; metaphors of, 19

death, 18, 27, 43–7, 87, 169

Democracy in the Streets, 70

188

Index

142; lesson, 145; questions, 110; war,
114
intertextuality, 20, 26
Israel, 75
Italians, 119, 138

Jackson, George, (black revolutionary author,) 101–2, 159, 170–1
Jewish: background, 72, 76; child, 159;
Christian relations, 38, 47; middle
class, 170; secular orientation, 72, 75;
religious training, 75; upbringing, 75;
women teachers, 4, 9, 15, 27, 69–
105, 107; *see also* anti-semitism, swastikas, Zionism
Jewish tradition: pragmatism and, 74–6;
progressive politics, and, 75–6; socialism and, 75–6, 169
junior schools, *see* schools
Justice Department, 126

Kennedy, President John F., 9
Kent State University, national guard
shootings at, 3, 103
kindergarten, *see* schools
King, Martin Luther, Jr., 131, 142–3,
145, 159
kinship, fictive, 131
Kozol, Jonathan, 144, 159, 164–5
Ku Klux Klan, 126, 128

labor: agricultural, 115; as working for
wages, 90; as central organizing concept, 90; conditions of teachers', 92–
95; domestic, 116–8; history, 8, 16–
7; language of, 90, 170; manual and
mental, 99, 117; movements, 91; of
love, 8; surplus, 98
language: as terrain of struggle, 158;
Bakhtin, 19–28; definition of, 3; of
Catholic church, 32; of kinship, 51;
of labor, 170; of pragmatism, 74; of
religious belief, 30–1, 40; of social scientific analysis, 40; politics and, 3,
164–5; problems, 133; racial contestation over, 113; *see also* discourse, vocabulary
languages: intersection of, 21, 112; multiplicity of, 201; of curriculum, 19; relationship between black and white,

110–2; social, 3; spatial coexistence
of, 21; temporal simultaneity of, 21
Larkin, Janey (character in children's
book), 9
left: distinguished from Left, 174; history of American, 70–1; -of-center,
140; scholars, 11; traditions of, 156;
-wing, ?; academic tradition, 91; organizations, 71; politics, 12
Left: distinguished from left, 174; in
eighties, 72–3; in fifties, 83; language
coopted, 22; New, 4, 70–1, 82, 107;
Old, 4, 70, 80; political potential of,
10; projects, 27; self-naming, 73; vocabulary of, 89
liberal, 14, 73, 134
life histories, *see* histories
loopholes, 141
Lortie, Dan, 10
Louisiana, 119, 130
love, 8, 42, 47, 54–6, 65, 116, 148–9,
151; *see also* care, nurture
lynching, 123

mall, shopping, 150–1
manual labor, 99, 117
Mardi Gras, 120–1, 141
Marx, Karl, 90, 156, 175
Marxist: -Christian project, 37; concepts, 90; discourse, 158, 175; projects, 174; self-naming, 73–4; theory,
90, 175, and practice, 156; tradition,
23, 27, 82, 160; *see also* Left
masquerade, racial, 144
master, white, 141, 147, 150
maternal metaphor, 148, *see also*
mothers
metaphors: 7, 24, 27, 48, 70, 169–70,
174; architectural, 62; central controlling, 20, 90, 109; deconstruction of,
167; implicit, 90–1; maternal, 148;
military, 70; paternal, 55; social contexts of, 165–6; for specific examples,
see: Catholic church, Communist
Party, communities; curriculum; family; house; identity; self; school; student; teacher; terrain; vocation;
women; *see also* emblematic, symbols;
methodology, 4, 7–28
Mexicans, 119

Index

Index

landscape, 64; meaning, 165; relations of research, 4, 12; text, 165; value of work, 93

social class: cross- perspective, 57; curriculum, 102; lower, 56, 133; middle, 56, 114, 159; origin, 93; professional middle, 12; race and, 109; ruling, 158; significance, 124; status, 161; teachers', 16; upper, 56; "yuppies," 56

socialism, 158

socialist: politics, 73–4; struggle, 169; tradition, 74; vision of labor, 90

sociology, 16, 133

Soelle, Dorothee, 155–6

South, 115, 129, 131

South Africa, 119, 152

southern belle, 123

Southern Democrats, 78

Spencer, Dee Ann, 10, 25

spirituals, 144

Sputnik, 3, 23

state, 65, 105, 125, 134, 161, 163; as terrain of struggle, 158; conservative restructuring of, 163; social service functions of, 163; *see also* government

stereotypes, 25, 48, 65, 84, 114, 117, 119, 127

strikes: farm workers, 9; sheetmetal workers, 8; students, 103; teachers, 8, 74, 100–1, 146

student: activism, 78–84; as political apprentice, 96, 100–5; council, 103–4

students, 2–4, 9, 30, 34–5, 42–4, 49–50, 52–4, 57–8, 78–80, 93–5, 100–5, 124–6, 131, 136–51, 161–2, 165, 172

Students for a Democratic Society (SDS), 71, 80–3

subjective, 12, 26, 165

subjectivity of researcher, 107

subversive organization, 80

summoning, *see* interpellation

swastikas, 88, 159

Sweet Honey in the Rock, 152

symbolic: code, 144; family, 169; matrix, 131, 147; mode, 165; representations, 90; terms, 143; system, 134

symbols: Christian, 58; church, 55; plantation, 114–6, 127, 136; racial segregation, 120; *see also* emblematic, metaphors

"talking back," 112, 127–8, 142

teacher, metaphors of: as artisan, 22, 90–1, 96, 100, 104; as author, 4, 105; as child, 92; as female worker, 168; as journey-person, 94–5; as mother, 22, 109, 165, 168; as professional, 23, 92; as worker, 8, 22, 91, 168; nature as, 35

teachers: becoming, 34–35, 84–88, 129–31; black women, 4, 9, 15, 27, 107–53, 171–4; Catholic women religious, 4, 26–7, 29–67, 107, 168–9; denigrated, 10, 27, 29, 108; groups, 15, 168; Jewish women, 4, 9, 15, 27, 69–105, 107; racial, 97–8; researcher's parents, 8–9; typical, 159

teachers' employment: attrition, 108; conditions of labor, 16, 92–95; firing, 142; hiring, 135–40; laid-off, 104; pregnancy, 138–9; professional expectations, 92; proletarian experience, 92; proletarianization, 170; resignation, 102; substitute, 93–5; strikes, *see* strikes; unions, *see* unions; wages, 8, 88–90

teachers' relationships: to administrators, 8–9, 19, 43, 53–4, 92, 126–7, 139, 142–4, 146–7, 150; to school boards, 8, 136, 138–9; to students, 2, 5, 8–9, 30, 35, 42, 50, 52–4, 57–8, 94–5, 100–5, 131, 136–51, 161–2, 165

Teachers for a Democratic Society (TDS), 86

Teachers' Lives and Careers, 25

teaching: as craft, 91, 170; practice, 137; relationship to political action, 10

terrain: alien territory, 135; identity as, 158; metaphorical description of, 61; schools as, 158; social landscape, 64; state as, 158; threshold of church, 63

theory, 7, 8; abstract, 162; critical, 91; dominant, 91; Marxist, 90, 175, and

Index

practice, 156; relationship to methodology and politics, 10
Thompson, Paul, 11, 24
tracking, 83
tradition, 5, 22, 74, 11, 118–9, 134, 152, 156–7, 165
triumphalism, *see* conservative
Trotskyist, 71, 80
Tuskegee Institute, 125

underground railroad, 134
unions: sheetmetal workers, 8; teachers, 10, 100, 146, 151, 153, 163, 168, 170; tenants, 84
universities, *see* colleges
uplift of the (black) race, 4; *see* also raising the (black) race
Upward Bound, 101
Urban League, 109, 152
usine (factory), school as, 100

Vatican II, 3, 41
Vietnam: curriculum, 97–100; summer, 80; war, 3, 9, 79, 81, 86, 88, 100, 149
Vietnamese, 149
vocabulary: educational, 83; ethical, 47; familial, 56; Left, 89; normative, 47; unconventional, 31

vocation, 58–60, as listening heart, 58–9

war: anti-war activities, 149; anti-war days, 86; anti-war demonstrations, 89; anti-war march, 79; anti-war movement, 81; childhood experience of, 65; Gulf war 155; peace rally, 104; *see also* military, Vietnam
Warner, Sylvia Ashton, 95
Washington, Booker T., 125
Washington, D. C., 78–9
"We shall overcome" (song), 142
welfare mothers, 84, 134
West, Cornel, 36, 38, 168
Willis, Paul, 10
"womanist," 117, 173
womanhood, cult of true, 123
women, metaphors of: as architects, 63; as builders, 63; as demolition workers, 63–4; as historians, 72–3
women's movement, 70, 72, 102; *see also* feminism
women's studies, 150
work, *see* factory, labor
Work and Revolution in France, 170
worldview, 3, 25–27, 164–6

Zionism, 75